THE
HEART 200 BOOK

Thomas A. Christie
&
Julie Christie

Other Books by
Thomas A. Christie

Liv Tyler: Star in Ascendance

The Cinema of Richard Linklater

John Hughes and Eighties Cinema

Ferris Bueller's Day Off: The Pocket Movie Guide

The Christmas Movie Book

Notional Identities

The Shadow in the Gallery

The James Bond Movies of the 1980s

Mel Brooks: Genius and Loving It!

The Spectrum of Adventure

A Righteously Awesome Eighties Christmas

Contested Mindscapes

John Hughes FAQ

The Golden Age of Christmas Movies

THE HEART 200 BOOK

A Companion Guide to Scotland's Most Exciting Road Trip

Thomas A. Christie
&
Julie Christie

EXTREMIS
publishing

The Heart 200 Book: A Companion Guide to Scotland's Most Exciting Road Trip by Thomas A. Christie and Julie Christie.

First edition published in Great Britain in 2020 by Extremis Publishing Ltd.,
Suite 218, Castle House, 1 Baker Street, Stirling, FK8 1AL, United Kingdom.
www.extremispublishing.com

Extremis Publishing is a Private Limited Company registered in Scotland (SC509983) whose Registered Office is Suite 218, Castle House, 1 Baker Street, Stirling, FK8 1AL, United Kingdom.

A CIP catalogue record for this book is available from the British Library.

ISBN: 978-1-9996962-1-4

Typeset in Goudy Bookletter 1911, designed by The League of Moveable Type.
Printed and bound in Great Britain by IngramSpark, Chapter House, Pitfield, Kiln Farm, Milton Keynes, MK11 3LW, United Kingdom.

Dedicated to
our beloved grandparents,
in memory of all those unforgettable
Sunday afternoon car trips.

HEART
200

THE ROUTE

Cairngorms National Park
Bruar
Blair Atholl
B8079
Killiecrankie
Tummel Bridge
B8019
Pitlochry
Loch Tummel
A9
Kinloch
Rannoch
A827
Ballinluig
B846
Grandtully
The Snow Roads
Fortingall
Aberfeldy
A923
Kenmore
Dunkeld
Blairgowrie
A827
Stanley
A93
Killin
Loch Tay
A9
Scone Palace
Glencoe
A85
Lochearnhead
Comrie
Crieff
A85
Loch Lomond
& The Trossachs
National Park
Loch Earn
Perth
A822
Muthill
A9
River Tay
Dundee
A912
St Andrews
Strathyre
A84
B827
Dunning
M90
Auchterarder
Kilmahog
Gleneagles
Braco
Trossachs Pier
A821
Callander
A823
Glendevon
A84
Doune
Dunblane
B919
A81
A873
Kinross
A911
Aberfoyle
Bridge of Allan
A91
B996
B9097
Loch Lomond
M90
A811
Stirling
River Forth
Falkirk

Contents

THE HEART 200 BOOK

A Companion Guide to Scotland's Most Exciting Road Trip

Thomas A. Christie

&

Julie Christie

Introduction

WRITING this book has been a labour of love for us, as we both live and work within the Heart 200 route and our business, Extremis Publishing, is based in Stirling where the route begins (though really your journey can start and end wherever you want it to). We are so fond of this area, and we hope that by visiting it you will come to feel the same way. It is a place which boasts history and culture, fun and excitement, unique experiences and more than a few funny wee stories along the way.

If you are planning a trip on the Heart 200 route, our advice is that you take your time, enjoy a leisurely approach, and come back time and again to appreciate everything the route has to offer. On top of the main destinations discussed in this companion guide, there are so many incredible places of interest which, even though not part of the main route itself, will fascinate and delight travellers. This book is purely intended to give you a taster of some of the attractions that you can seek out along the route, but there is so much more to see and do – it's up to you to find all of the hidden gems that are scattered so liberally throughout this wonderful area.

In addition to the main route, there are a number of extra sub-routes around the region which extend from each section of the Heart 200. These invite you to explore further, and see more of Scotland in the process. To find out more about these sub-routes, we would invite you to visit the official Heart 200 website at *www.heart200.scot*. As you will discover, it is not simply a core route of 200 miles, but actually a collection of well over 200 attractions – many of which you will read about in the following pages.

No organisation or individual paid an advertising fee to be mentioned in this book, and the views expressed within are our own. We've tried to strike a good mixture of things to see and do, some of them free and open all year round, and others which will charge an admission fee and may only have seasonal opening hours. So please remember to check the various websites ahead of time to confirm entry charges to the attractions as well as to verify their availability at the time of your trip. This guide does not discuss hotels, restaurants or shops unless they are historically or culturally significant, simply because there are so many of them along the route. But if you visit the Heart 200 website, you will discover up-to-date information about accommodation, places to eat and the many interesting and eclectic retail outlets which exist throughout the area.

A very big vote of thanks to all the people who we met along the route, who are too numerous to mention here. Many of them provided us with information about their attractions, and relayed some of the fascinating tales which help to make this area the wonderful place it is. They took time out of their busy schedules to talk with us during our travels, and we thank them for agreeing to be involved.

Stirlingshire and Perthshire are areas of great natural beauty, and we would ask anyone visiting to help take care of our environment and to treat the communities you encounter with kindness and respect. That way, when we welcome your return to the area it will still look as beautiful the next time you are here.

Though it is an unofficial publication, this book has been written with the full approval and co-operation of the Heart 200 team, with special thanks to Managing Director Robbie Cairns for his great patience in answering all of our questions! This book would not have been possible without our occasional travelling companions Mary Melville, Eddy Bryan, Amy Leitch and Ian McNeish – all of whom brought their characteristic good humour and eye for detail to the journey. We owe you all an ice-cream... or perhaps even a fish supper!

If you enjoy yourself half as much as we did while researching and visiting all of the villages, towns and cities that are along the Heart 200 route, we have no doubt that you will have a great time on your travels. We hope that you will take pleasure in undertaking what is, in our opinion, Scotland's most exciting road trip.

Tom & Julie Christie
Stirling, February 2020

Chapter One

The City of Stirling

WHILE you are free to start your Heart 200 journey at any location around the route, there is no better place to begin your journey than the ancient city of Stirling. Known throughout Scotland as the 'Gateway to the Highlands', Stirling is an historic city with a thoroughly modern eye on the world. Every year, visitors flock to the area to see its blend of ancient heritage and vibrant contemporary attractions for themselves.

Stirling has been settled since prehistoric times, with several Bronze Age and Iron Age discoveries around the city and its surrounding area. With its location as the lowest bridging point on the River Forth, it has been one of the most prominent settlements in Scotland for centuries. King David I declared Stirling a Royal Burgh in 1130, and

it has been the site of numerous significant historical conflicts including the Battle of Stirling Bridge in 1297 and the Battle of Bannockburn in 1314. Stirling became an important international trade hub, and it remains proud of its long mercantile heritage. While it has long been well-known around the world for the part it played in the Wars of Scottish Independence and the Jacobite Rising of 1745, as well as being the ancient seat of the Royal Stuart dynasty, today it remains an important centre for higher education, retail, industry and tourism. Queen Elizabeth II granted Stirling the status of a Royal City in 2002, the year of her Golden Jubilee.

Though arguably best-known for its famous castle and many historical monuments, Stirling offers something for just about everyone – whether your interest is in arts and culture, Scottish history, exploring new places, or even a spot of retail therapy!

Stirling Castle

Dominating the city's skyline on its ancient basalt crag is the commanding sight of Stirling Castle (*www.stirlingcastle.scot*). One of Scotland's largest and most historically significant castles, it is hugely popular with visitors every year. A royal residence since at least the 12th century, it was the ancient administrative hub of Stirling. Eventually becoming the royal seat of the Stuart dynasty, the castle underwent significant architectural expansion under King James IV and James V. Surrounded on three sides by steep cliffs, the castle's strikingly elevated location and robust defensive position are obvious to visitors even now.

Stirling Castle has been besieged numerous times over the centuries, the most recent being in 1746 when Bonnie Prince Charlie made an unsuccessful attempt to take control of the castle during the Jacobite Rebellions. Its form has changed dramatically over the centuries, with the overwhelming majority of its current buildings dating from

between 1490 and 1600 due to construction ordered by Stuart kings; the varied European influences of the fascinating architecture indicates the international aspirations of monarchs such as James IV, James V and James VI.

Today, the castle remains remarkably well-preserved, and guests can visit its courtyards, Great Hall, Chapel Royal, and the beautifully-restored Royal Palace. There is an exhibition dedicated to the famous Stirling Heads – carved wooden portraits of Scottish nobility and other figures, originally created during the Renaissance – while meticulous recreations can now be seen in their vibrantly-painted glory on the ceiling of the King's Presence Chamber within the Royal Palace. The Regimental Museum of the Argyll and Sutherland Highlanders (*www.argylls.co.uk*) is located in the King's Old Building, and details the Castle's proud military past. Because of its authentic period architecture, Stirling Castle's expansive esplanade has served as an open-air concert venue for a range of high-profile performances by artists which have

included REM, Wet Wet Wet, Bob Dylan and Runrig. Used as a military parade ground in years past, it is now the location of the Castle's annual Hogmanay celebrations every 31st December.

In addition to its historical importance, Stirling Castle has also been a popular filming location for many movies and TV series over the years. They have included:

- *Kidnapped*, a star-studded adaptation of Robert Louis Stevenson's perennially popular novel – directed by Delbert Mann and starring Michael Caine and Vivien Heilbron – which appeared in cinemas in 1971 and featured extensive filming throughout Scotland including scenes shot in Stirling (most especially around Stirling Castle) as well as Killin.
- John Henderson's 2005 retelling of the Greyfriars Bobby story, *The Adventures of Greyfriars Bobby*, which featured performances by Gina McKee, James Cosmo and Sir Christopher Lee, and included filming around Stirling's Old Town and the grounds of Stirling Castle. The location of the Old Town Cemetery in Stirling stands in for Greyfriars Kirk Yard, and the famous Church of the Holy Rude can also be seen in some shots.
- The exteriors and title sequence of the famous BBC series *Colditz*, originally broadcast between 1972 and 1974, were filmed at Stirling Castle, which doubled for the infamous *Schloss Colditz* World War II prisoner of war camp.
- The legendary Sir Alec Guinness was rarely on better form than when playing Major Jock Sinclair in Ronald Neame's 1960 post-war drama *Tunes of Glory*. This Oscar-nominated film showcased the historic exterior of Stirling Castle.
- The darkly comic historical tale *Burke and Hare*, directed by John Landis and released in 2010, featured Simon Pegg and Andy Serkis as the eponymous body-snatchers, with various scenes for the film shot at Stirling Castle.

Kings Park

The ancient Kings Park (*www.stirling.gov.uk/planning-building-the-environment/the-environment/parks-in-stirling/kings-park*) was, as its name suggests, originally founded as a royal pleasure ground in the 12th century, when it was used for aristocratic pursuits such as jousting and hunting. Today, everyone can enjoy the park, and it is one of Stirling's best-used recreational areas. Many activities take place there, with facilities including swings, trampolines, a tennis court, a floodlit wheelie park for bikes and skateboarding, and a range of outdoor gym equipment. For those who prefer more serene pursuits, there is a peace of mind garden within the park, as well as picnic tables with seating.

Kings Park is a popular location for walkers, with a comprehensive path network allowing for a number of different trails which allow for some stunning views of the surrounding area, such as Cambusbarron, Gillies Hill and Bannockburn. On the far side of Stirling Golf Club, just off Dumbarton Road, is the King's Knot – a large sculpted earthwork which was once part of Stirling Castle's formal gardens. Remodelled over the centuries, the King's Knot rises to 3 metres at its highest point, and as well as making for a pleasant walk it also affords an impressive aspect of the Castle itself.

The National Wallace Monument

Opened in 1869 and designed by John Thomas Rochead (1814-78) to commemorate the life of Sir William Wallace (1270-1305), the National Wallace Monument (*www.nationalwallacemonument.com*) stands on the Abbey Craig overlooking Stirling and is one of the city's most prominent landmarks.

Standing 67 metres high and constructed in the Victorian Gothic style, the monument also contains a statue of Wallace on one of its corners which was created by sculptor David Watson Stevenson (1842-1904).

The shoulder of the Abbey Craig, where the monument is situated, is said to be the location where Wallace observed King Edward I's army assembling prior to the Battle of Stirling Bridge in 1297. The tower consists of four levels, each of which contains a separate hall showcasing different exhibits such the famous "Hall of Heroes", which encompasses busts of noteworthy Scots from history including John Knox, George Buchanan, Sir Walter Scott and Thomas Carlyle.

The Wallace Monument is famous for having a number of artefacts on display which are thought to have belonged to William Wallace, but by far the most celebrated has been the remarkable Wallace Sword – a two-handed longsword measuring 1.63 metres and nearly 3 kilograms in weight. This must-see exhibit is alone worth climbing the 246-step stone spiral staircase in order to view a unique part of Scotland's historical heritage for yourself.

Climbing the staircase culminates in arriving at an observation level at the very top of the building which affords a stunning panoramic view of the city and its outlying districts. Looking at Stirling and the surrounding area from the pinnacle of the Wallace Monument is one of the most impressive experiences in Scottish tourism. You won't want to miss the incredible sight that awaits you there.

The Stirling Smith Art Gallery and Museum

First opened to the public in 1874, the Stirling Smith has been at the centre of cultural life in Stirling for almost a century and a half. The Stirling Smith (*www.smithartgalleryandmuseum.co.uk*) is the museum and art gallery which serves the city, and is considered to be the single largest exhibition space in all of Central Scotland.

Situated on Dumbarton Road near the city centre, the Stirling Smith (which is still often referred to affectionately by its original name of 'The Smith Institute' by the city's locals) was originally established by the bequest of artist Thomas Stuart Smith (1815-69) to showcase his extensive collection of paintings, display contemporary artwork, and allow public access to a museum and library reading room. Over the years this mission has expanded considerably, with the Stirling Smith's collections now being regarded as among the most significant in Scotland and holding many artefacts of national and international importance.

The modern Stirling Smith building houses a museum, an art gallery and the Cunninghame Graham Library as well as a lecture theatre and very popular café area. Their permanent exhibition, 'The Stirling Story', recounts the history of Stirling from Neolithic times through to the present day and presents some extraordinary artefacts including an aeroplane propeller owned by Frank and Harold Barnwell (who were responsible for Scotland's first powered flight in July 1909), the Key to the City of Stirling presented to Bonnie Prince Charlie during the 1745 Jacobite Rising, and the axe used in the last beheading in Britain (the execution of the radi-

cals John Baird and Andrew Hardie in 1820). Perhaps most notably, the museum is also home to the world's oldest football (c.1540), originally discovered in the rafters of the royal residences at Stirling Castle during renovation work. The football is on permanent display in the museum, and has regularly been exhibited around the world. The Smith also houses the world's oldest curling stone (c.1511), a famous bust of Stirling's only Member of Parliament to have served as Prime Minister (to date), Sir Henry Campbell-Bannerman (1836-1908), and the extensive Neish Pewter Collection.

The Stirling Smith's huge collection of artwork has been painstakingly digitised by its expert curatorial team, and has been licensed over the years to some of the most prestigious organisations in the world. Lectures and public presentations are regularly given at the Smith, and local organisations meet on the premises regularly. Additionally, the Stirling Smith is unusual amongst cultural institutions in that it has its very own murder mystery novel, *The Shadow in the Gallery*, which is set

within the Smith and is on sale in the museum shop in aid of the upkeep of the building. There are also many activities for younger visitors, including the beautiful Ailie's Garden – a natural sensory space at the rear of the building which contains many activities and sights to enjoy.

The Albert Halls

One of Stirling's most popular entertainment venues, the Albert Halls (*www.stirling.gov.uk/tourism-visitors/attractions-events-venues/albert-halls/*) have been welcoming visitors for over a hundred years, with many public performances, concerts and conferences taking place within its capacious walls. Located near the city's shopping centre, on Dumbarton Road, the Albert Halls staff presents an ambitious line-up of events throughout the year with something to suit almost every possible taste.

In spite of its imposing historic exterior, the Albert Halls is a thoroughly modern and highly adaptable facility with a café bar on site, and hire of the main and lesser halls is available along with meeting room rental. Visitors will want to check in at the booking office to see what events are available during their stay in Stirling; from ballet to stand-up comedy by way of opera and tribute bands, there is never any shortage of variety.

Stirling Old Bridge

Situated amidst stunning scenery, Stirling Old Bridge – which spans the River Forth (*www.historicenvironment.scot/visit-a-place/places/stirling-old-bridge*) – is an astonishing example of mediaeval stonemasonry, and still one of the finest in Scotland today. Built in either the 15th or 16th century, the bridge replaced a number of timber predecessors (including that which was involved in the 1297 Battle of Stirling Bridge) and is 82 metres long in total, comprising four arches. At the time of its construction, it was the largest bridge in Scotland and one of the most strategically important

crossing points in the country. As Stirling Burgh Archaeologist Dr Murray Cook points out in his book *Digging into Stirling's Past* (2019), many famous figures from history have crossed it over the centuries including Mary Queen of Scots and Robert Burns. Famously, one of the arches of the bridge was removed by General William Blakeney (1672-1761) during the Jacobite Rising of 1745 in order to impede Bonnie Prince Charlie's army as it marched southwards. Today, the bridge is pedestrianised and its historical significance makes it a popular destination for visitors to the town.

The Bastion

One of Stirling's most surprising secrets comes in the form of the Bastion (*www.thistlesstirling.com/events/the-bastion*); an historical exhibition based around a 16th century Scottish jail, which lies beneath the Thistles Shopping Centre. (Access to the Bastion is via spiral staircase from the main shopping area above.) Free of charge to visit, this entertaining mini-museum was fully renovated in 2018 and is always worth a visit thanks to its focus on the macabre world of bygone crime and punishment. This unusual 'Thieves' Pot' has a long history, dating from when it was a defensive tower which was part of the Stirling Burgh Wall. With a combination of exhibits and detailed interpretation boards, to say nothing of its infamous 'bottle dungeon', why not come along and delve into its shadowy secrets for yourself?

The Battle of Bannockburn Visitor Centre

Previously known as the Bannockburn Heritage Centre, the Battle of Bannockburn Visitor Centre (*www.nts.org/uk/visit/places/bannockburn*) is dedicated to bringing Scottish history alive. As its name suggests, the Centre focuses on the two-day battle in 1314 between King Robert the Bruce and King Edward II which was to become one of the most pivotal moments in Scotland's history. Set amongst an area of beautifully-maintained parkland, the Centre contains an immersive 3D visitor experience which boasts many interactive features. There is an emphasis not just on the tactics and outcomes of the famous Battle of Bannockburn itself, but also the many historical figures who took part in it.

Robert Burns visited Bannockburn in 1787, and the experience moved him to the extent that he was inspired to write one of his most famous and patriotic poems, *Scots Who Hae* (1793). The battle is also referred to by Roy Williamson (1936-90) in the lyrics of his famous song *Flower of Scotland* (1967), and it has inspired artwork by artists as varied as John Duncan, John Phillip and Eric Harald Macbeth Robertson.

The Battle of Bannockburn Visitor Centre is located on Glasgow Road, Whins of Milton. Due to high visitor demand, pre-booking your ticket by contacting the Centre in advance of your visit is recommended. In addition to its exhibitions, many events organised by the National Trust for Scotland take place on the premises throughout the year. The building

also contains a gift shop and café area. The expansive grounds feature a medieval 'physic garden', a memorial cairn and the modern Bannockburn Monument. Whenever you should visit, make sure that you take the time to view the imposing Bruce Memorial Statue, designed and commissioned by acclaimed sculptor Pilkington Jackson (1887-1973) and created in bronze by Thomas Taylor Bowie (1905-96).

Cambuskenneth Abbey

Constructed by King David I in the 12th century, Cambuskenneth Abbey (*www.historicenvironment.scot/visit-a-place/places/cambuskenneth-abbey*) was an Augustinian monastery founded to serve Stirling Castle which was originally known as the Abbey of St Mary of Stirling. Because of its proximity to the city, it was once among Scotland's most significant abbeys and enjoyed numerous royal visits over the years. It eventually became the

burial place of King James III and Queen Margaret of Denmark in the 15th century, before later falling into neglect following the Scottish Reformation. While the ruins of the Abbey are worth visiting for the historical interest alone – the building was the site of King Robert the Bruce's parliaments at various points in the 14th century – the jewel in its crown is the bell tower which still stands today. Comprehensively restored in 1859, this 13th century campanile gives some indication of the monastery's now-bygone architectural grandeur. Open to visitors between April and September, the Abbey is situated just off Ladysneuk Road – a short drive from Stirling city centre. The interior of the tower is as incredibly well-preserved as its exterior, and is an essential destination for any Scottish history enthusiast.

Cowane's Hospital

A 17th century almshouse in the city's Old Town, Cowane's Hospital (*www.cowanes.org.uk*) was founded in 1637 from the bequest of prominent Stirling merchant John Cowane (1570-1633). The building was later converted into the Guildhall of the city's Merchant Guildry. Located on Stirling's historic St John Street with substantial surrounding gardens, Cowane's Hospital has become a vibrant arts venue which is currently available to be hired for private events. Its long history with the Merchant Guildry also continues to this very day, as the organisation continues to host events on the premises. It is a Category A listed building, and considered one of the finest examples of its type in Scotland. The grounds contain one of Scotland's oldest bowling greens, dating back to the 18th century. Cowane's Hospital Trust is the second-oldest surviving charitable trust in Scotland, and is still

supporting people in Stirling even in the present day. According to local legend, the building's famous statue of its founder John Cowane – lovingly known among Stirling residents by the nickname of 'Auld Staneybreeks' ('Old Stony Trousers') – miraculously comes to life, jumps from his stone pedestal and dances in the building's courtyard every Hogmanay.

The Church of the Holy Rude

Constructed in the 12th century by King David I as the parish church of Stirling, the Church – or 'Kirk' – of the Holy Rude (*www.holyrude.org*) is the second-oldest building in the city after Stirling Castle. Its current structure was developed in the 15th century, with its chancel and distinctive tower later being added in the 16th century. Situated on St John Street near the Castle, several royal coronations and baptisms took place in the building (including the crowning of King James VI in 1567 by Bishop Adam Bothwell of Orkney, with John Knox delivering the sermon), and it remains an active place of worship under the auspices of the Church of Scotland even today.

As well as its many exquisite stained glass windows (many of which date from the late 19th century), produced by some of the country's most celebrated experts such as Daniel Cottier & Co., the church building also has a long and fascinating history. Perhaps most infamously, this includes its interior being bisected by a dividing wall from the 17th century until 1936 due to a congregational schism. The church itself was founded in 1129, but its early structure was destroyed by a fire in 1405. The rebuilt construction's architecture was expanded over the centuries until it began to resemble the building we know today.

The church also boasts an impressive fine oak beam roof, uncovered during its restoration in 1940. It has the distinction of being one of only three surviving churches in the United Kingdom which, though still serving a modern-day congregation, are historical sites of royal coronations. (The other two, Westminster Abbey and Gloucester

Cathedral, are located in England.) Entry to the church is free, and the dedicated welcome team have a wealth of knowledge concerning the building and its heritage which they will share with you upon request.

The Old Town Cemetery

One of the most historically important cemeteries in all of Scotland, the Old Town Cemetery (*www.oldtowncemetery.co.uk*) lies adjacent to Stirling Castle and contains the final resting places of some of the country's most noteworthy historical figures. The Cemetery is actually divided into a number of sections which include the original me-

dieval cemetery, the Drummond Pleasure Grounds, the modern Snowden Cemetery, and – perhaps the most significant of all – the Valley Cemetery, which was established by the Victorians. Taken collectively, these peaceful grounds are home to some exceptional sights including the instantly-recognisable Star Pyramid Memorial, constructed in 1863 by stonemason William Barclay to commemorate the lives of the Drummond family of seed merchants and publishers, which is currently considered to be Scotland's largest pyramid.

The Old Town Cemetery is the resting place of many noteworthy historical figures, several with significance far beyond Stirling or even Scotland. Graves on the site include those of merchant John Cowane (founder of Cowane's Hospital), Britain's first female professional archaeologist Christian Maclagan, and the Solway Martyrs. Guides are available locally which give information about the details and locations of various noteworthy resting places. A walk through the expansive grounds of the Old Town Cemetery is considered to be one of the city's most instructive and meditative journeys of exploration.

Mar's Wark

One of the greatest historical curios of Stirling, Mar's Wark (*www.historicenvironment.scot/visit-a-place/places/mars-wark*) is a Renaissance mansion situated on Mar Place. Though only the derelict façade survives in the modern day, this huge townhouse was one of the most impressive structures in all of Stirling when constructed in the late 16th century. It was built by John Erskine (?-1572), Earl of Mar, who was the keeper of Stirling Castle; the mansion's title, Mar's Wark (literally 'The Earl of Mar's Work'), keeps his memory alive centuries later.

Mar's Wark was so grand in its day that it was used to entertain royalty; King James VI was known to have stayed there as a guest. Over the years the house's fortunes waned and it eventually became a workhouse, though it was later revived for use as a barracks during the Jacobite Rising of 1715. Some years later, when Bonnie Prince Charlie besieged Stirling Castle in 1746, Mar's Wark lost its roof in the course of the explosive conflict and subsequently fell into ruin. Though only its imposing frontage now endures, it remains a fascinating relic of Stirling's grand architectural past.

The Old Town Jail

Open between July and September, the Old Town Jail (*www.oldtownjail.co.uk*) is a living monument to law and order in historic Stirling. First opened in 1847 as a penitentiary when the old jail at the Tolbooth became too overcrowded to adequately fulfil its purpose, the building was eventually converted to a military prison before eventually becoming a museum.

This conscientiously-maintained jailhouse on St John Street retains its period features, and was extensively renovated in the 1990s. Today it is considered one of Stirling's top-rated tourist attractions, and with good reason. The Old Town Jail has become renowned for its elaborate performance tours and tales of numerous characters from Stirling's past, including hangman Jock Rankin and infamous outlaws from history – ranging from petty criminals and murderers to political prisoners and campaigning reformers.

The building also features an observation tower which offers an impressive view of the Old Town and the lands which lie beyond it. On a clear day, visitors can see as far as the Ochil Hills and even the beautiful Trossachs National Park. Guests are advised to check opening times in advance of their visit.

The Tolbooth and Mercat Cross

Located right at the heart of Stirling's ancient settlement, Broad Street was the nucleus of the city for centuries, and the hub at its heart was the Tolbooth (*www.stirling.gov.uk/tolbooth*). This was the site of law and order for the city, and numerous public executions took place here throughout history. While Stirling's Tolbooth has existed for centuries, the current building – which is situated between Jail Wynd and Broad Street – was constructed in the early 18th century at the design of Sir William Bruce (1630-1710) and was extended numerous times, culminating in the addition of a

courthouse and jail in 1811. The building was greatly admired for its clock tower, though its jail became infamous as having the worst conditions in Britain at the time; it was closed in 1847, and its inmates transferred to the then-newly constructed Old Town Jail. Stirling town council continued to meet in the Tolbooth until 1875.

In the present day, the Tolbooth has become one of the city's most significant venues for the performing arts, including live music and dramatic productions amongst numerous other aspects of Stirling Council's Heritage and Cultural Services.

The building also houses a recording studio. Many different events run throughout the year, and the Tolbooth has also become a popular location for private and corporate events as well as wedding ceremonies. Its auditorium seats 200 people, and the building also houses a bar and restaurant as well as a public foyer, rehearsal space and meeting rooms.

The centre of Broad Street is also the location of Stirling's ancient stone Mercat Cross (*www.instirling.com/sight/mercat.htm*). During the time of the Stuart monarchs, the Old Town – which had gradually expanded below the Castle after Stirling was declared a Royal Burgh in the 12th century – was a thriving hub of merchant activity, and the Mercat Cross was the epicentre of the city's trading activity. It stands proximate to the site of the Tolbooth – the city's one-time administrative and organisational centre. The Mercat Cross has become famous for its 'puggy': the eye-catching unicorn figure which is on its apex.

Stirling Golf Club

Stirling has a very long history with the game of golf, with resident monarchs known to have partaken in a round from time to time when distracting themselves from their royal duties. History records King James IV taking part in a game of golf as far back as 1505, and nowhere is the city's proud sporting heritage more obvious than at the prestigious Stirling Golf Club (*www.stirlinggolfclub.com*).

Situated in Kings Park, on Queen's Road, Stirling Golf Club is one of the most celebrated golf courses in Central Scotland. Founded in 1869, the club was eventually expanded to a full 18-hole layout in 1904 and was then extensively redeveloped in the 1960s. The course boasts stunning views of the surrounding area, with beautifully-maintained parkland scenery complementing its verdant fairways.

Stirling Golf Club is a member of the internationally-renowned James Braid Reciprocal Association. In addition to the Club's main playing facilities, there is also a bar and restaurant on site as well as a pro shop. Anyone planning to take part in a golfing trip or visitor group bookings should contact the Club in advance.

Argyll's Lodging

Constructed in the 17th century in close proximity to Stirling Castle, the stately Argyll's Lodging (*www.historicenvironment.scot/visit-a-place/places/argyll-s-lodging/*) is arguably the city's most famous town house. The historic residence of the Earl of Stirling and, subsequently, the Earls of Argyll, the building was designed in the Renaissance style and is considered highly significant amongst architectural historians. Over the years it would become a military hospital, a youth hostel, and – from 1996 – a museum, with the house's rooms being decorated and furnished in line with its historic past.

Today, it is easy to see why this striking mansion was once the home of noble families and used to entertain royalty. Beyond its majestic façade, Argyll's Lodging contains many outstanding features including reconstructed tapestries, an intricate decorative chair of state and elaborate painted decoration which has been scrupulously preserved for the enjoyment of future generations.

This grand property, located on Castle Wynd and maintained by Historic Environment Scotland, is only open to the public at certain times of year, but even its meticulously-conserved exterior is worth a visit. Anyone hoping to view its impressive interior should check the HES website ahead of their trip to ensure availability of public access via guided tours.

St Ninians Old Parish Church Tower

The clock tower of St Ninians Old Parish Church in Kirk Wynd, St Ninians (*www.canmore.org.uk/ site/46227/stirling-kirk-wynd-st-ninians-old-parish-church*), is all that now remains of a historical church building which dates back to the 11th century – and possibly earlier. During the 1745 Jacobite Rebellion, the church was used by the Jacobites to store gunpowder, and in January 1746 these supplies were detonated during the retreat of Bonnie Prince Charlie's army, almost completely destroying the church in the process (though whether this happened intentionally or accidentally remains a matter of contention amongst historians!). While some fragmentary ruins of the church remained, the clock tower survived the blast; it had been rebuilt only a few decades earlier, in 1734, on the site of a much earlier structure.

Following the Jacobite withdrawal, the tower building eventually became unsafe and access to the surrounding graveyard was restricted. However, in the late 20th century extensive restoration work took place which was funded by Historic Scotland, donations from the local community and also the current St Ninians Old Parish Church which stands adjacent to the site. The tower's steeple is home to a 16th century bell, while its clock was replaced in 1901. The tower's classical architectural influence and its undeniable historical importance make it a popular location for visitors to Stirling; while the graveyard is not always accessible to the general public due to ongoing conservation work, the tower is a prominent sight for some distance and if necessary can be admired in some detail from the perimeter wall.

The Engine Shed

Built between the late 1890s and early 1910s as part of a military complex near the banks of the River Forth, the Engine Shed (*www.engineshed.scot*) was originally used for the maintenance and repair of steam locomotives near the rapidly-expanding Stirling Railway Station. Located on Forthside Way, the building subsequently fell into disrepair when the armed forces departed Forthside in 1990. However, the structure has since been comprehensively renovated and extended, and in 2017 the Engine Shed was reinvented as Scotland's Building Conservation Centre – a hub for building and conservation professionals, as well as the general public.

At the heart of the Engine Shed's mission statement is a desire to help the public to find new and innovative ways to explore their built heritage. This includes everything from advice on how to help preserve and care for traditional structures all the way through to tutorials on building materials and combating common problems encountered in the upkeep of older and historical properties.

The Engine Shed offers events, seminars, learning programmes, building advice, and a series of changing exhibitions. They also have comprehensive information available in the form of publications on the subject of building restoration and preservation, while their instructional and informational events run all the way through the year. Checking their constantly-updated website before your visit is highly recommended, due to the sheer range of different events that are on offer at various times.

Stirling Gin Distillery

Opened in the Spring of 2019, Stirling Gin Distillery (*www.stirlinggin.co.uk*) is based in the historical 19th century Old Smiddy at Lower Castle Hill. Stirling Gin was born in October 2015 when Cameron and June McCann distilled their first bottle to mark the occasion of their 26th wedding anniversary. Their gin soon proved to be so popular that a larger still was required, and demand grew so rapidly that Stirling Gin is now a spirit that is recognised throughout Scotland and beyond.

Built close to Stirling Castle, the Old Smiddy is thought to be constructed on the site of King James V's horse stable in the 16th century. The building's distinctive Victorian façade has been sensitively preserved, but the Old Smiddy is now home to a thoroughly modern distillation facility which also houses a visitors' centre and shop. Their services include gin tours, tasting sessions, masterclasses, and many other events throughout the year.

Stirling Gin Distillery offers an innovative membership package, and a very wide-ranging variety of spirits are available for purchase. For more information of the company's history, its range of products and its seasonal events, a visit to their website is highly recommended.

The Beheading Stone

Standing atop Stirling's historic Mote Hill like a macabre sentinel, the ancient Beheading Stone (*www.stirling.gov.uk/tourism-visitors/places-to-visit/the-beheading-stone*) is a popular historical destination for anyone taking the scenic Back Walk footpath route which circles Stirling Castle and the walls of the city's Old Town, though it can also be easily accessed from Crofthead Road. The stone itself is protected by an iron canopy, placed on a plinth for public display. Though it is a peaceful place to visit now, the Beheading Stone was once the site of numerous executions that were ordered by Scotland's royalty throughout the centuries.

Today the site is arguably best-known for the beheading of Murdoch, Duke of Albany in 1424 at the order of King James I on a charge of attempted high treason. As Dr Murray Cook mentions in his 2019 book *Digging into Stirling's Past*, Stirling's historic place of execution was so well-known by the 19th century that it inspired Sir Walter Scott to reference it in his famous poem *The Lady of the Lake* (1810) – a work which was to attract many tourists to Stirling at the time.

The Old Arcade

An historic gem in Stirling's city centre, the Old Arcade (*www.stirlingarcade.com*) was first built in 1881 to serve a Victorian clientele. Extending between Murray Place (near Stirling Railway Station) and King Street, the arcade was a thriving centre of retail in its day, housing two hotels (the Temperance Hotel and the Douglas Hotel), around forty shops, several residential apartments and the famous Alhambra Theatre. The Alhambra had an impressive interior, and presented performances by many of the top music hall talents of the time, before eventually being converted into a cinema. By the time of the Second World War, the Alhambra was closed down, though in more recent years part of the theatre has been renovated and reopened by its present proprietors.

Stirling Arcade underwent extensive refurbishment throughout the 20th century, and many of

its period features have been carefully restored including the concourse's glass roof. With four-storey facades marking the entrances at either end of its central walkway, the arcade remains an impressive sight. Its owners, along with Stirling Local History Society, have worked together to present a permanent exhibition of the arcade's history, with many photographs and personal mementos illustrating the story of this unique complex.

Today the Old Arcade houses a number of independent shops, restaurants and bars, and offers a fantastic atmosphere for locals and visitors alike. Checking out their website for a list of current retailers is highly recommended, as the arcade hosts an eclectic range of stores to suit many tastes.

Made in Stirling

Operated by Creative Stirling, Made in Stirling (*www.creativestirling.org*) is the city's exciting arts collective and a flourishing hub of creative industry where there is always something interesting going on. Made in Stirling is a popular destination in the city's King Street, and features a wide range of artworks which have been created by artists, sculptors, musicians and authors from the local area. In addition to items for sale, the hub also features a number of workshop spaces and an expansive gallery area, with regularly changing exhibitions and an all-embracing assortment of creative and arts-based events.

With a firm ethos of diversity and inclusion, Made in Stirling is dedicated to presenting the very best of arts and creativity from the city and its surrounding area. This friendly and welcoming environment has become widely admired among local people as well as tourists and sightseers. Consulting their website and/or social media channels before your visit is always a good idea, due to the fact that there are so many different presentations, events and courses taking place at the hub.

Made in Stirling is also home to Stirling City Radio (*www.stirlingcityradio.com*), which is the city's acclaimed digital radio station. Stirling City Radio is popular with listeners not just in the local area, but far beyond thanks to their streaming

online broadcasts and mobile app. With a mixture of interviews, regional news and great music, there is always something of interest to listen to. So why not tune in to their live transmissions before your visit to Stirling, to get an idea of what's going on in this vibrant city before you even get there?

The Peak

The nucleus of Stirling's sports village, The Peak (*www.the-peak-stirling.org.uk*) is a leisure centre with a difference. Located at Forthside Way, The Peak offers activities to suit all abilities – and a mindboggling array of sporting choices. Though it has become especially well-known for its ice rink, which has played host to curling tournaments and is home to the Scottish National Curling Academy, The Peak also features a swimming pool, health suite, gymnasium, fitness and dance studio, a number of outdoor pitches, and the rewarding challenge of an 11-metre high climbing wall.

Many activities take place at The Peak, from walking sessions through to racquet sports, and the centre is always well-attended. In addition to all of the various sporting pursuits, members of the public can also enjoy the well-regarded Village Café and Village Lounge which offer snacks, meals and drinks throughout the day. The Lounge is especially enjoyed amongst spectators due to the fact that its observation windows overlook skating and curling events taking place on the ice rink below.

For information about the many activities taking place at The Peak, including admission prices and membership offers, please check out their website before your visit. They also have a very active social media presence, with a well-populated YouTube channel showing some of their sports and leisure pursuits in action.

Blair Drummond Safari Park

Based between Stirling and Doune at Lime Avenue, Blair Drummond, the Blair Drummond Safari Park (*www.blairdrummond.com*) is easily accessed from the city and has become one of Scotland's most popular independently-run tourist attractions. It has been owned and operated by the Muir family ever since it first opened in 1970. The park is perfect for nature lovers everywhere, and a visit there presents many opportunities to view animals ranging from giraffes, big cats, elephants, meerkats, birds of prey, and many others.

Blair Drummond features many unique highlights which really set it apart. Their macaque 'drive-thru' is the only one of its kind in all of Scot-

land, and was used as the location for the BBC's *Peter Kay's Car Share* sitcom in 2017 when lead characters John and Kayleigh visit a safari park. Furthermore, Blair Drummond's chimpanzees live on their own island – one which can only be visited by boat. With 400,000 visitors to Chimp Island every year, the boat trip (which is included in the entry price to the Park) has become one of the busiest foot passenger services in Scotland.

The Blair Drummond Safari Park also features a pirate ship with a remarkable secret – it is an actual seafaring ship! It was previously used as a ferry to Eigg in the Western Isles, but after its decommissioning it was rescued from the scrapyard and transported all the way to Blair Drummond, where it has been delighting visitors ever since.

The Park plays a major role in breeding programmes for many endangered animals, including the red ruffed lemur and the southern white rhino. They are part of the Endangered Species Breeding Programme, a global network which cares for rare

species of animal. They actively support conservation projects not just in Scotland, but throughout the UK and across the world.

Many events take place at Blair Drummond Safari Park throughout the year, so planning your visit ahead of time is recommended – not least as there is always so much to see and do. In addition to their education programmes (which have made the Park a popular destination for school trips) and their online shop, there is even an annual pantomime which takes place in December. The Park itself closes to visitors over the winter months, so checking their website for availability during your visit to Stirling is suggested. The site also includes details of Blair Drummond's admission fees and membership packages.

Duncarron Medieval Village

Situated at Carronvalley Forest in the Carron Valley, a short drive from Stirling, the breathtakingly accomplished Medieval Village at Duncarron (*www.duncarron.com*) is one of the most exciting open air museums in Scotland. The brainchild of the CEO of the Clanranald Trust for Scotland, Charlie Allan, Duncarron Medieval Village is a painstakingly-constructed, historically-correct representation of a 13th century fortified Scottish village, built in consultation with respected architectural and historical experts to provide the greatest possible authenticity. The result is a spectacular achievement, where visitors are not only invited to experience the sights of medieval Scotland but also

come into contact with its realistic sounds, smells, feel and taste.

The Duncarron Medieval Village experience has been conceived with the idea of helping guests to immerse themselves fully in the Scotland of long ago, before modern technology. It has thus rapidly become a truly unique place to deliver instruction about Scottish history, culture and customs – though the appeal of Duncarron goes far beyond its educational potential. The project has been used many times since its inception in 1995 as a location for TV and film productions, while its team – Combat International – have become a highly-respected name in movie-making, appearing in over 200 productions for the big and small screens so far. The project counts A-List Hollywood star Russell Crowe as one if its most high-profile friends, going back to Charlie Allan having worked closely with him during the filming of Ridley Scott's historical epic *Gladiator* (2000).

Duncarron Medieval Village also has its own folk band, Saor Patrol (*www.saorpatrol.com*), who travel all over Europe and have played live at many festivals in order to raise money for the project. The band is made up of volunteers from the Clanranald Trust for Scotland, and plays Celtic Rock music on the Great Highland Bagpipe, drums and electric guitar. They have produced a number of albums, and continue to tour widely.

The Village is now open to the public, and its dedicated team of staff and volunteers work tirelessly to provide an unforgettable experience for their visitors. They offer a full programme of events throughout the year, and have spent more than £2.5 million at time of writing on the project – an especially noteworthy achievement given that the entire amount has come from donations and the

efforts of hard-working volunteers, with no government funding having been received to date.

Visitors to Duncarron Medieval Village will be met by an incredible living history team who are

committed to bringing history alive for guests. They are hugely enthusiastic about their work, having appeared on TV features including *Secret Scotland with Susan Calman* in 2019. Just like the Scottish heroes of yesteryear, the staff members are larger-than-life characters – quite literally, in fact, as operations manager Finn Allan is 7 feet and 1 inch tall!

Duncarron Medieval Village has it all – the people, the knowledge, the props, the replica weapons, the facilities, and the passion for history that can only mean one thing – memories that all the family will treasure. As well as a set location, the village is also increasingly in demand for medieval banquets, special ceremonies including weddings, social events, corporate entertainment, and much more besides. For opening hours and admission prices, as well as details of forthcoming events and other news, please visit the website for all of the village's latest information.

Chapter Two

The Wooded Western Edge

NOBODY expected to encounter Monty Python on the Heart 200, but the legendary comedy team filmed at Doune Castle during the production of *Monty Python and the Holy Grail* – and, in more recent years, the same historic venue has become one of the most sought-after filming locations in Scotland. But that's just one of the surprises in store for you in this beautiful part of the country. The Wooded Western Edge of Heart 200 features some stunning scenery, including locations around beautiful Loch Lomond and the Trossachs, boat trips at picturesque Loch Katrine, walks around charming, historic Callander, exciting activities in verdant Aberfoyle, and much more besides.

This section of the route contains some of the most striking vistas in all of Central Scotland,

and there are plenty of places to keep all the family interested – from physical activities through to gentle walks and many historical locations to discover. Whether you are an animal lover or an aficionado of unique and unusual retail destinations, there will be something surprising for you to uncover along the way. Prepare to expect the unexpected!

Doune and Deanston
Doune is a burgh of Stirling which offers an impressive range of things to see and do – some of them quite surprising. Lying within the parish of Kilmadock and surrounded by the River Teith and Ardoch Burn, Doune has a rich history and was visited by Bonnie Prince Charlie when he passed through the town in 1745 during the Jacobite

Rising. In the past, Doune was famous for its fire-arm manufacturing, and it is believed that the first shot in the American War of Independence was fired from a pistol made in Doune. While the town no longer produces firearms, examples of its pistol-manufacturing days are greatly sought after by collectors and are often to be found in museums.

Doune's history is also accompanied by abundant folklore, with ancient tales of faeries in the area. This mythology centres around three sites: Ternishee (from the Gaelic *tir na sídhe*, meaning 'Faery Land'), which is a small copse of trees situated east of Annat Chapel; Tullochanknowe, a burial mound near the Bridge of Teith; and the Fairy Knowe, a knoll situated on the bank of the Ardoch Burn. Folk tales of faeries are common in the Celtic tradition, and local legend has it that these mystical creatures can sometimes be witnessed in the aforementioned areas near the town.

Due to its lengthy history as a settlement, in more recent years Doune has become of particular interest to archaeologists thanks to the discovery by Headland Archaeology of a Roman fort thought to date back as far as 79AD. Yet the area was settled long before this point, as a burial cist (a type of stone coffin) was uncovered during quarrying which revealed the body of a child which is believed to date back to the early Bronze Age: approximately 1800BC.

The town is particularly well-known for the extraordinarily arresting sight of Doune Castle (*www.historicenvironment.scot/visit-a-place/places/doune-castle*), a remarkably-preserved courtyard castle. Situated on Castle Hill, it is thought to have been originally constructed in the 13th century and then heavily damaged during the Scottish Wars of Independence, leading to it being rebuilt – in its current form – at some point in the 14th century by the Duke of Albany, Robert Stewart (1340-1420), who was the Regent of Scotland between 1388 and 1420. The castle became the property of the crown in 1425 and was subsequently employed as a royal hunting lodge until becoming the property of the Earls of Moray in the 16th century. Doune Castle was later to be involved in military action in the 17th century during the Wars of the Three Kingdoms and Glencairn's Rising, and then during the Jacobite Risings of the 17th and 18th centuries. This would take its toll, for by 1800 the castle was without a roof and in a state of ruin. It remained in this derelict state until restoration work took place in the 1883 and again in 1970. The Earl of Moray committed the castle to the nation in 1984, and it is now in the care of Historic Environment Scotland.

Due to its amazing degree of preservation, the castle is a must-see attraction for any visitor to Doune. Among its most popular features are the grand courtyard, the astonishing views from the battlements across the Teith towards Ben Lomond, and the Lord's Hall – a splendid hall which has been beautifully restored with timber panelling and floor tiles, as well as many other historical flourishes recalling the grandeur of the past. The adjacent Great Hall – which is a remarkable 66ft by 26ft, with a height of 39ft (that is, 20m x 8m x 12m) – has become a popular venue for wedding parties in recent years. The highest point in the castle, the Lord's Tower, is 95ft tall (approx. 29 metres).

Doune Castle has been influential to a number of works of literature, including the anonymously-authored 17th century ballad *The Bonnie Earl o' Moray* and Sir Walter Scott's historical novel *Waverley* (1814). Today, the castle is a regular highlight of film location tours due to its imposing presence and attractive location. Doune Castle has been host to numerous productions including:

- HBO's global phenomenon *Game of Thrones*, its eight-season epic adaptation of George R.R. Martin's fantasy novel cycle *A Song of Ice and Fire* which ran between 2011 and 2019, saw its pilot episode filmed at Doune Castle, which was used as the site of Castle Winterfell – the location of the family home of House Stark, later to become one of the pivotal settings in the entire series. (When *Game of Thrones* was picked up for a full series, the location filming for Winterfell took place at Castle Ward near Strangford in County Down, Northern Ireland.)

- Graham Chapman's King Arthur kicks off his infamous search for the Holy Grail from Doune Castle in the memorably surreal 1975 British comedy classic *Monty Python and the Holy Grail*, directed by Terry Gilliam and Terry Jones.

- Starring Sandy Welch as Robert the Bruce and Brian Blessed as King Edward I, Bob Carruthers and David McWhinnie's *The Bruce*, a 1996 account of the Scottish King's life, involved location filming at Doune Castle as well as at Crieff's Drummond Castle.

- The subject of Robert the Bruce was also addressed by David MacKenzie's 2018 film *Outlaw King*, which starred Chris Pine, Tony Curran and Stephen Dillane. Doune Castle is employed as Douglas Castle in the film, and is even seen being engulfed by fire – albeit that the resulting inferno was achieved using special ef-

fects, meaning that the real castle was never in danger of harm during the production.

- The BBC's lavish, internationally co-produced miniseries adaptation of Sir Walter Scott's famous historical novel *Ivanhoe* (1819), starring Steven Waddington and Victoria Smurfit, was first broadcast in 1997 and featured scenes filmed around Doune Castle. The castle had also appeared in an earlier adaptation of *Ivanhoe*, this time for cinema, in 1952. Directed by Richard Thorpe for MGM Studios, it starred Elizabeth Taylor and Robert Taylor.
- Doune Castle has also been a key location in Starz Inc.'s hit TV series *Outlander*, which started its highly successful run in 2014. Starring Caitriona Balfe, the series is an adaptation of Diana Gabaldon's popular novel cycle, and Doune Castle is used as the basis for the fictional Castle Leoch, which is the home of the Clan MacKenzie in the 18th century.

Doune Castle is a well-attended venue throughout the year, and visitors are advised to check the website for opening times and admission charges – as well as any special events – before their planned arrival.

On the scenic approach to Doune is the impressive and imposing Sir David Stirling Monument (*www.undiscoveredscotland.co.uk/doune/stirling-memorial*), located on the Hill o' Rou – adjacent to the B824. This is an attention-grabbing statue which was sculpted as a memorial to the late Colonel Sir David Stirling, OBE, DSO (1915-90),

who founded the Special Air Service (SAS). Sir David was a Scottish landowner and keen mountaineer, whose soaring reputation was cemented by his distinguished service to the Allied cause in World War II. The statue is thus sometimes referred to locally by the alternative name of 'the SAS Memorial'.

Another famous Doune attraction, the Argaty Red Kites Project (*www.argatyredkites.co.uk*) is a reserve and feeding station for wild birds based at Lerrocks Farm, Argaty, and was the winner of the RSPB Nature Tourism Award 2018. This centre is the only feeding station for red kites in all of Scotland, and features a hide where members of the public can watch these wonderful birds, which were reintroduced to Central Scotland by the RSPB and Scottish National Heritage. There is also a visitor hub on site, with comprehensive information about the red kites and the other wild birds of Scotland.

Lerrocks Farm is situated on the Braes of Doune, and against this scenic background the hides provide a unique opportunity to view the beautiful red kites in comfortable surroundings without any risk of disturbing their day-to-day activities. The kites are fed on a daily basis, and other types of bird are regularly attracted to the conservation area including kestrel, peregrine, hen harriers and buzzards.

In 1998, the first red kite chicks were hatched in Central Scotland for over a century. The Project suggests that the best time to see these magnificent birds in high numbers is during the autumn and winter months, when they come together to form large roosts. Farm tours are also available, which include not just the sight of the red kites but also red squirrels and visits to historic archaeological sites which include Heather Jock's House and Gallow Hill. The Project draws attention to the amazing effect of red squirrel moulting, which starts from their head and then moves

through to the tail which results in some amazing and unexpected fur colouration during the process. Also, the farm's ponds are home to all eleven species of dragonfly and damselfly that an observer could expect to find in Scotland.

Detailed information about the conservation of the red kites' population, and many other fascinating facts besides, are provided to visitors when they come to Lerrocks Farm. Because the Argaty Red Kites Project is situated on a working farm, it is advisable to call in advance to arrange your visit. Their website also includes many other useful details, including photography tips and travelling directions to Lerrocks Farm.

For those seeking a memento of their visit to Doune, the Scottish Antiques and Arts Centre (*www.scottish-antiques.com*) is based on the Carse of Cambus near Doune and offers a wide range of interesting and often unanticipated items for sale. Established in 1999, the centre has become a very popular venue for its range of antique and vintage items: three halls of goods are available for perusal, ranging from jewellery and ornaments to artworks, print and media, and era-specific items. The centre also offers contemporary shopping, including local produce and confectionary. Along with a range of seasonal events, there is also a farmer's market which takes place on a monthly basis at the Courtyard, which showcases locally-produced artisan food and plants. A bistro-style restaurant, Café Circa, is also situated on the premises.

Stirlingshire and the Trossachs are home to some majestic hill walks and mountain experiences, and anyone seeking to make the most of the area's incredible natural beauty – particularly if they are new to the area – may wish to seek the expert advice of the Doune-based Tagit Mountain Guides (*www.toughtags.co.uk/products/trossachs-mountain-guides*). Experienced mountaineer Dr Jon Cluett, who has an academic background in the environmental sciences, offers professional guiding services for everything from walks in the lowland countryside through to the challenges of multi-pitch rock climbing and winter mountaineering. Based in the area since 1998, Jon also offers mountain activity consultancy services as well as training sessions on a range of topics. Anyone intending to undertake a hillwalking or mountain climbing experience during their stay in the area may want to consider contacting Jon via his website to find out

more about his booking availability and the costs of his various guiding services.

Anyone looking to find out about the many different places of interest in Doune, as well as the numerous events which take place throughout the year, would be advised to pay a visit to the conveniently-situated Kilmadock Information Centre (*www.doune.co/home/visit/kilmadock-development-trust-and-information-centre*) which is located in the town's Balkerach Street. Operated by the Kilmadock Development Trust, the information centre contains information about all aspects of Doune and the surrounding area including maps, valuation rolls, census data, and a range of material regarding local tourism, local history and walks in the area. There is also a range of books on Scottish subjects, and many other items including gifts.

An excellent destination for a family day out is the lively Briarlands Farm and Fun Centre (*www.briarlandsfarm.co.uk*), based near Doune at Blair Drummond. Located in stunning scenery, Briarlands Farm is the perfect place for outdoor activities. There is an extensive list of things to see and do, including tractor rides, a zip wire, sand-pits, go-karting, play frames, a sheep pen maze, archery, animal feeding, and a range of arts and crafts pursuits. And this is just scratching the surface! Adults may prefer the tearoom, where a wide range of food from local suppliers is served, and also the opportunity to pick and buy your own strawberries (depending on the time of year that you visit). Consulting the farm's website before your trip is always a good idea, due to the fact that there are a number of seasonal events taking place through the year that might coincide with your visit.

Eight miles north of Doune, situated just along the A84, the historic Deanston Distillery (*www.deanstonmalt.com*) features an informative visitor centre which takes its visitors on a journey through the centuries from the building's early days as a cotton mill through to its current use as a modern distillery. As well as the famous tours of the premises, there is also their 'Warehouse 4 Experience' to enjoy, where whisky can be tasted straight from the cask. There are a number of tours available, including the Classic Tour, the Tasting Room Tour, the Heritage Tour, and the Whisky and Chocolate Tour.

The current distillery building on Teith Road was opened in 1785 as the Deanston Cotton Mill, designed by famous Industrial Revolution figure Richard Arkwright (1732-92). The mill prospered, and as the workforce grew there was need for greater accommodation in the surrounding area. In 1813, it became the first village in Scotland to use gas lighting (some 45 years before neighbouring Doune), and in 1830 a lade and waterwheels were fitted to the mill building. By 1949, electrical turbines were installed to provide hydroelectric power from the River Teith. The mill closed its doors in 1965, but the building was subsequently converted to a distillery with the first bottle of Deanston Highland Single Malt Scotch Whisky

being produced in 1974. The visitor centre opened in 2012, and today Deanston Distillery is among the best-known in all of Scotland. As well as its considerable range of products for sale, Deanston Distillery is also home to a popular café where food is prepared by hand in their acclaimed distillery kitchen.

There are many unique facts about Deanston Distillery which set it apart. It is the producer of the oldest annual release of organic whisky in the world, and is 100% self-sufficient on account of its generation of hydro-electricity. Though the building was initially powered by one of the largest waterwheels in Europe at the time, it was later replaced by turbines in 1949 designed by David Brown, at that point the owner of Aston Martin. Deanston operates using traditional methods, with no automated processes. One highlight is its open-top mash tun, which is the largest of its kind – and only one of six in all of Scotland which operates open-topped. All Deanston whisky has natural colouring and is bottled un-chill filtered, meaning that it retains all of its natural oily qualities – a must for true whisky aficionados.

Deanston also has a claim to fame in popular culture, in that the distillery's distinctive architecture has attracted producers of films and TV series to use it for location filming. In particular, the village appeared in Ken Loach's drama *The Angel's Share* (2012) and the BBC's miniseries *Rillington Place* (2016), as well as in season 2 of *Outlander* where the distillery was used to portray a wine warehouse in the French port of Le Havre. The distillery has had many famous visitors, including Hollywood star Leonardo di Caprio who was a guest during what has been, to date, his only visit to Scotland.

Also on the River Teith is the striking sight of the historic Bridge of Teith, a crossing on the A84 near Doune. This bridge was built by Stirling's Robert Spittal FRSE (c.1800-52), the royal tailor, in 1535, and replaced a ferry which had pre-

viously been the main mode of transport over the river.

Near Doune and Deanston is Mains Farm wigwam holidays and helicopter glamping (*www.mainsfarmwigwams.com*), based in the charming rural village of Thornhill. With astonishing views over the Carse of Stirling all the way to the Hills of Fintry, Mains Farm is the perfect place for anyone seeking to enjoy walking or cycling around this area of amazing natural beauty. Mains Farm offers camping with a difference – visitors can choose to stay in a heated, double-glazed and insulated wigwam (complete with plug sockets, lights, kettle and fridge), or one of the Lux Family Wigwams which offer a little bit of glamping extravagance due to extras such as foam mattresses, mini-kitchen area and double-glazed patio doors. The wigwams are all made in Scotland with wood sourced from sustainable forests.

However, Mains Farm's main claim to fame in recent years has been its Royal Navy Sea King helicopter, transformed into one of Scotland's most exclusive holiday locations. With a mini-kitchen and even a shower room on board, the helicopter provides a luxury glamping experience like no other. With a bed situated in the helicopter's tail and its cockpit seating area specially angled towards the breathtaking Carse of Stirling, the Sea King is an unforgettable destination for a holiday experience, and its renovation featured in an episode of Channel 4's *George Clarke's Amazing Spaces*. More recently, the Sea King has been joined at Mains Farm by a Twin Pioneer plane. Built in the 1960s in Prestwick and originally used by a pilot training centre, the fully renovated Twin Pioneer is sure to be a similarly inimitable holiday destination for fans of quirky getaways and aviation enthusiasts alike.

Among the many other attractions in Doune are Doune Ponds (*www.scottishlandestates.co.uk/ helping-it-happen/case-studies/doune-ponds-doune- community-woodland-group-and-moray-estates*), a local nature reserve near the town which offers some wonderful walks around a network of pathways. Situated on the site of an old quarry, just a few hundred yards from the town centre, Doune Ponds are managed by Doune Community Woodland Group. The unstinting efforts of the volunteers in maintaining the site has won the group the Scotland's Finest Woodlands Award at the Community Woodlands Awards in 2017, and their endeavours were again Highly Commended in 2019.

Callander and Kilmahog

A picturesque and busy town which features many independent shops and eating places, Callander is considered the eastern gateway to Loch Lomond and the Trossachs National Park. Situated on the River Teith, the town is always popular with walkers and cyclists and features many well-liked trails in the area including Bracklinn Falls Bridge and the Callander Crags, Ben A'an, Loch Lubnaig, the River Keltie, and Loch Venachar. Bicycles can be hired for trips from local businesses such as the Wheels Cycling Centre (*www.incallander.co.uk/ wheels_cycling_centre*) and CNDo Outdoors Scotland (*www.incallander.co.uk/cndo-outdoors-scot- land*), which offers instructional courses on outdoor walking, though it is always advisable to check their websites ahead of time to check availability of services, especially outside of the tourist season. With cycle trails and footpaths covering areas such as the old Callander to Oban railway and a section of the Rob Roy Way (*www.robroyway.com*), Callander is the perfect place for wildlife watching, sightseeing, or just enjoying a walk in stunning natural scenery.

Newcomers to Callander will want to pay a visit to the Visitor Information Centre based in the Main Street (*www.incallander.co.uk/visitorcen- tre*), which is open throughout the tourist season and features the latest news of events taking place in the town as well as details of many of the attractions that can be visited in Callander and its surrounding area.

Views of masterful Ben Ledi dominate this historical town, which has been occupied since Neolithic times. It was used by the Romans as a fort, known as Bochastle, in the 1st century. Centuries later, a battle was fought near the town in 1646 with the Campbells of Argyll led by Campbell of Ardkinglas on one side of the conflict and a force of Athollmen on the other. Callander had further military significance in the 18th century, when Major William Caulfeild (1698-1767) was charged with constructing a road here in 1743 as part of a wider network which was employed by the Army during the later Jacobite Rising. Decades later, the town became popularised as a tourist destination – in no small part thanks to the work of appreciative literary visitors such as Sir Walter Scott and William Wordsworth. With the arrival of the railway in 1858, Callander's standing as a sightseeing destination was cemented, and the town remains a very popular location for visitors today. In 2018 it was recognised as Scotland's first Social Enterprise Place due to the exceptional degree of high quality social enterprise activity taking place in the town.

In Ancaster Square is one of Callander's most eye-catching landmarks, St Kessock's Church. It is named for a saint and disciple of Saint Columba (521-97), who is known to have preached in the area during the 6th century. Though it has not been active as a place of worship since the mid-1980s, this remarkable Gothic building (constructed in 1883, replacing an earlier church on the site thought to date back to the 12th century) features a prominent spire and remains a commanding focal point in the town centre.

An unusual feature of the town is the Neish Heads – stone carvings of human heads which can be seen on the façades of some buildings within the town. According to local history, the heads have

an interesting (if bloody) tale to tell. In the Battle of Boltachan, which took place in the hills to the north of St Fillans in 1522, the McNab Clan of Killin defeated the Neishes of Neish Island in Loch Earn. The vanquished members of the Neish Clan were decapitated and their heads taken back to Killin by the triumphant McNabs. The surviving Neishes did not forget this battle, and almost a century later – in December 1612 – they ambushed a McNab caravan in Glen Lednock heading for Killin. This prompted the McNabs to attack Neish Island in retribution, killing all but two of the residents (a boy and a girl, who escaped the bloodbath). Thus the remainder of the Neish Clan's heads were returned to Killin to join those of their fallen comrades from decades beforehand. In the years which followed, Callander eventually became a McNab town, and the carved heads of fallen Neishes were placed on buildings as a stark warning to what happened to enemies who opposed the Clan. At least six of these heads can still be seen today around Callander. Can *you* find all of them?

Among the many things to see and do in Callander is the fantastic Hamilton Toy Collection (*www.thehamiltontoycollection.co.uk*) on Main

Street, a museum of childhood memories which also features a well-stocked shop full of delightful cult curiosities. One of the largest privately-owned toy collections in the whole of the UK, this treasure trove of rarities and playthings from yesteryear truly has to be seen to be believed. While the collector's shop alone contains many happy memories for toy-lovers and pop culture enthusiasts of all generations, the museum showcasing the toy collection – which is presented over two levels – is packed to bursting point from floor to ceiling with curiosities and beloved playthings of yesteryear.

The museum was started by Philip and Patsy Hamilton, and the collection is now maintained by their children Cris and Catriona Hamilton along with Catriona's husband, John Hunter. During the Second World War, when rationing was at its height, young Philip Hamilton would swap home-grown strawberries from his family's garden in exchange for lead soldiers – some of which are now

on display in the collection among an estimated 6,000 others. (It is claimed that nobody has ever been brave enough to try counting every single soldier in the huge collection!) Over the years, the collection grew and grew, with the Hamiltons developing a keen eye for amazing toys of all kinds. When the family moved from Croydon to Callander, their combined collection of toys filled five shipping containers – and this included none of their own furniture or personal items. Even now, they have a family tradition of exchanging toys as gifts for Christmas and birthdays. On one occasion, a member of the family was stopped by customs at a Spanish airport and their bags thoroughly searched due to the discovery of wires and suspicious metal items during a routine X-ray examination. The customs officials were stunned to discover an extensive collection of rare, recently-purchased Spanish Scalextric cars in the bags, which are now presented in the museum for the public to see.

The Hamilton Toy Collection is a true gem of Callander that is not to be missed. The shop and museum is open to the public on a seasonal basis, so it is advised to check their website or social media channels ahead of your visit to be sure of availability of admission and current entry fees.

Callander High Street also features a well-regarded antiques shop: Lady Kentmore's Antiques (*www.ladykentmores.com*). The shop has been a finalist in the BBC Home and Antiques Best Antiques Shop in the UK Competition, and has a wide range of ornaments, jewellery and rarities on offer. Beyond the fine porcelain and *objets d'art*, however, Lady Kentmore's specialises in unusual and sometimes unexpected collectables including fairground antiques and medical curiosities. Visitors should prepare to encounter some genuine surprises when browsing! The shop is also home to a small museum and a display with audio-visual elements which focuses on the life of outlaw and folk hero Rob Roy MacGregor (1671-1734).

The celebrated Trossachs Distillery Ltd. (*www.mcqueengin.co.uk*), situated at The Barn, Upper Drumbane on the outskirts of Callander, is a multiple award-winning distillery which is the home of McQueen Handcrafted Gin. The distillery shop is open throughout the week, but tours must be booked online in advance. Tours are generally organised for a maximum of eight visitors; to arrange a group tour for a larger number of people, the company should be contacted ahead of time.

The initial idea for McQueen Gin was born in 2015 when husband and wife Dale and Vicky McQueen – an engineer and chef respectively – enjoyed a gin and tonic in their garden one day, and decided to combine their technical skills and culinary talents to open their own distillery. Work began the following year on the McQueen Gin distillery, with the company's first still – 'Little Maggie' – arriving in the April of 2016. On their first day of trading, the McQueens launched four world-first gin flavours in the form of Sweet Citrus, Mocha, Smokey Chilli and Chocolate Mint. With the first guests arriving to enjoy the McQueen Gin Distillery Experience, two new varieties of gin were introduced: McQueen Super Premium Dry and Spiced Chocolate Orange Gin.

Since those exciting and productive early days, McQueen Gin has gone on to ever greater success. Their state-of-the-art distillery, which has been named 'The Robert McQueen Building', was officially opened by Scotland's First Minister Nicola Sturgeon MSP in May 2019. The distillery building, which is a cutting-edge facility, was once a milking parlour farm building, while the exact location of the McQueen Gin headquarters was previously the game larder for Cambusmore Estate – a National Reserve renowned internationally for its wildlife. The McQueen family, respectful of the natural environment, use recyclable glass bottles across their entire range. The McQueen Gin research and development facility has been christened 'The Ginnovation Bothy', and is the launchpad for brand new breakthroughs in gin advancements.

The McQueen Gin Experience offers members of the public the opportunity to explore the atmospheric distillery and gain first-hand experience of how these award-winning gins are made. Eagle-eyed visitors will notice from the commemorative notices that the stills have been named in honour of the McQueens' beloved pets 'Big Doogy' and 'Little Maggie'.

Callander is also host to a number of festival events which run at various points throughout the year, including the largest rural jazz and blues festival in Scotland, a Summer Festival, and a Winter Festival. It additionally offers a popular cinema (*www.incallander.co.uk/cinema*) based at Callander Hostel and operated by Callander Film Society. For a schedule of forthcoming features and admission costs, please visit their website. Anyone seeking leisure activities will want to check out the excellent McLaren Leisure Centre (*www.mclarenleisure.co.uk*), which offers a swimming pool, fitness suite, sauna and steam room, soft play area, and much more besides. Details of admission fees are available online.

Situated near Callander is the Castle Rednock Trekking Centre (*castlerednocktrekking.com*) at Castle Rednock Farm in Port of Menteith, which offers a wide range of outdoor services including quad pods, pony trekking, Segway trekking and orienteering, as well as Shetland Pony driving. Activities are available to suit groups, individuals and families, as well as corporate events, so booking ahead is advised. Callander is also home to a fa-

mous golf club (*www.callandergolfclub.co.uk*), first opened in 1890, which is home to some truly beautiful parkland views as well as the prospect of challenging and enjoyable play.

The town is additionally well-known among TV buffs as being the setting for long-running BBC series *Dr Finlay's Casebook*. Starring Bill Simpson as the titular Dr Finlay, this long-running medical drama was based on A.J. Cronin's novella *Country Doctor* and was broadcast between 1962 and 1971. Filming took place in and around Callander, which portrayed the fictional 1920s town of Tannochbrae. The exterior of Dr Finlay's residence was filmed at Arden House (previously Auchengower House), which is located in Callander's Bracklinn Road.

The beautiful hamlet of Kilmahog, situated just half a mile away from Callander, is a picturesque village which over the years has become particularly well-known for its perennially popular retail destination, the Kilmahog Woollen Mill

(*www.simplythebestdestinations.co.uk/Scotland/o 8Kilmahog1*). Originally built in 1758 as a flax mill which produced the famous Kilmahog Rug, the building has been extensively renovated while still retaining its distinctive period features. The store offers a wide range of clothing and tartan items as well as souvenirs. Harris Tweed, a Clan tartan centre and Highland dress are all available on the premises, along with a popular restaurant. The adjacent field is home to some friendly and very distinguished Highland cows – don't forget to find out more about their story when you're visiting!

Another well-known retail destination in the village is the Trossachs Woollen Mill (*www.simplythebestdestinations.co.uk/Scotland/o 9%20Kilmahog%20(2)*) – the perfect destination for anyone seeking tourist gifts, clothing or a visit to the weaving shed, where visitor demonstrations show how the weaving process took place with historically-accurate machinery. A snack bar and coffee shop are also available. The nearby Scottish Real Ale Shop (*www.scottishrealales.com*), situated next to the Lade Inn near the centre of the village, will be every ale enthusiast's dream come true. Featuring no less than 210 different Scottish ales produced by over 40 individual micro-breweries (ranging from the Northern Isles to the Scottish Borders), there is bound to be something here to suit the taste of almost any ale enthusiast.

Kilmahog is a popular place for quiet walks alongside the River Leny (*Garbh Uisge* in the original Gaelic), given its location at the junction between the Lochearnhead and Trossachs roads. Remains of an ancient hillfort can be found at nearby Dunmore overlooking Loch Venachar, while the earthworks from Roman ramparts dating from the 1st century can be seen in the vicinity of the Bochastle area.

Kilmahog has an intriguing geographical claim to fame in the form of Samson's Putting Stone, a massive rock which was deposited by a prehistoric glacier at the summit of Bochastle Hill overlooking the town of Callander. The name of this glacial erratic derives from a local legend, namely that a family of giants had once organised a putting competition in the area and that one of their stones had been thrown too far, subsequently ending up permanently lodged atop the hill.

Aberfoyle

A village set in scenic environs, Aberfoyle is particularly treasured by outdoors enthusiasts and na-

ture lovers. There are many panoramic views and scenic trails to enjoy, including a gentle stroll to a nearby waterfall and more strenuous routes to lofty woods and rocky crags. Situated close to the picturesque Queen Elizabeth Forest, Aberfoyle is the perfect place for walkers and cyclists. Also popular is the charming and peaceful Doon Hill and Fairy Knowe walk (*www.walkhighlands.co.uk/lochlomond/doon-hill.shtml*): a circular route which boasts some truly beautiful views. Walkers undertaking the Rob Roy Way often find Aberfoyle to be an ideal stop between Drymen and Callander. The famous Three Lochs Forest Drive (*www.forestryland.gov.scot/visit/forest-parks/queen-elizabeth-forest-park/three-lochs-forest-drive*) is located close to the village; this national forest can be viewed from a 7 mile-long stretch of road which takes in the natural beauty of Lochan Reòidhte, Loch Drunkie and Loch Achray. Please note that the Forest Drive is closed to vehicles in the winter months; it is best to check the website for details of accessibility when planning your visit.

Aberfoyle takes its name from the Gaelic *Obar Phuill*, meaning 'Mouth of the Phuill Burn'. The village has a long history, dating back to being the location of a fortress built by Aedan, Prince of the Forth in the 6th century. Though well-known for its connections to Mary, Queen of Scots and Rob Roy MacGregor, it was also home to the Rev. Robert Kirk (1644-92), renowned for his translation of the Biblical Book of Psalms into Scots Gaelic as well as his famous book *The Secret Common-wealth of Elves, Fauns and Fairies* (1691). Kirk believed that nearby Doon Hill was a gateway to a mystical realm of faeries; the existence of such supernatural kingdoms was a common belief in old Celtic tradition. Like nearby Callander, the village became a popular tourist destination in the 19th century, and visitors could arrive by train from 1882 until 1951, when Aberfoyle Railway Station closed to passenger traffic (though it continued to operate freight services until 1959).

Aberfoyle's busy VisitScotland iCentre (*www.visitscotland.com/info/services/aberfoyle-icentre-p234571*) is situated conveniently on Main Street at the Trossachs Discovery Centre, and is an ideal first port of call for any visitor to the town. The knowledgeable staff members at the centre have in-depth information on many locations throughout the area. There is also a bookshop on the premises, along with other themed merchandise which will be of interest to visitors to the area.

For those who enjoy an outdoors challenge, Go Ape (*www.goape.co.uk/locations/aberfoyle*),

the famous outdoor activity centre, features two of Britain's longest zip-wires – something which gives aerial adventure enthusiasts the chance to view the beautiful forest scenery from an entirely different perspective! The Aberfoyle branch of Go Ape is company's largest adventure course in the UK, and based in the Queen Elizabeth Forest Park (located within the Trossachs National Park) it is one of the most incredible outdoor activity destinations imaginable.

Go Ape Aberfoyle has become renowned for its 'Treetop Challenge' – the monster challenge of high ropes adventures, which involves a 323 metre-long zip-wire ride before visitors can make their way back down from a 45 metre-high vantage point via a 426 metre-long wire. But it isn't all just high-wire stunts at Go Ape; the scenery is stunning, with waterfalls and woodlands forming a jaw-dropping natural backdrop to the action.

Visitors can expect an amazing time at Go Ape Aberfoyle; the compound is so huge, they use around 10 tonnes of woodchip a year for their landing sites alone. Their range of activities is very diverse, with something to suit just about any exercise enthusiast, so be sure to check out their website for more information on the kind of pursuits you can take part in when you visit. They were recently named the winners of the Scottish Outdoor Leisure Award for Best Outdoor Activity, with the prize being collected in person by none other than Duke – Go Ape Aberfoyle's famous gorilla mascot!

Located near Aberfoyle, Lodge Forest Visitor Centre (*www.forestryandland.gov.uk/visit/forest-parks/queen-elizabeth-forest-park/the-lodge-forest-visitor-centre*) is billed as the gateway to Queen Elizabeth Pass. The centre offers a variety of amazing trails which will meet all tastes, including the Oak Coppice Trail, the Waterfall Trail, the Lime Craig Trail and the famous Duke's Trail. Visitors will also find tree-top adventures available at the centre, as well as a café and plenty of information about the area. The Lodge Forest Visitor Centre is situated at the Duke's Pass, which is named for the Duke of Montrose who ordered construction of a road between the eastern shoulder of Craigmore and the old road at the Trossachs pass in 1885, making Aberfoyle an alternative route to the Trossachs. It was acquired by the Forestry Commission and made accessible to the public in 1931.

Go Country: The Forest Hills Water Sports Centre (*www.gocountry.co.uk*) is based at Kinlochard and offers plentiful activities such as canoeing, a water park and an assault course. Qualified instructors are on hand to offer advice, or alternatively visitors can hire their own equipment for the day. With corporate team activities and party packages on offer, the sky's the limit at Go Country: guests can take part in country sports, outdoor exploring or even cliff-jumping! Seasonal opening times and other details are available from their website.

Perfect for cycling enthusiasts, Aberfoyle Bike Park (*www.biketrossachs.org.uk/aberfoyle-bike-park.html*) provides no less than 700 metres of biking trails, with many unique features and gratifying challenges along the way. Located on Trossachs Road, Aberfoyle Bike Park has become one of the most popular biking tracks in all of Central Scotland, and is the perfect destination for people seeking a cycling experience either alone or as part of a team. For anybody seeking a different kind of outdoor activity, picturesque Aberfoyle Golf Club (*www.aberfoylegolf.co.uk*) is situated nearby at Braeval, at the foot of the Menteith Hills. Great for players with both high and low handicaps, this course was opened as a 9-hole course in 1890 and is widely considered to be one of the most charming in all of Scotland.

The acclaimed Scottish Wool Centre (*www.simplythebestdestinations.co.uk/Scotland/1 oAberfoyle*) is one of the most popular attractions in Aberfoyle, and presents many activities for visitors to enjoy. These include 'The Gathering', a three-times-daily dog and duck show (which takes

place between April and September), where a shepherd will give a history of Scottish sheep and commands his dog 'on hand' to herd ducks. Other animals are sometimes also on site in observation areas, including birds and different breeds of sheep. The Scottish Wool Centre also offers a large shopping area with a wide range of clothing and other gift items on sale, an extensive whisky and food hall, and a restaurant.

Based not far from Aberfoyle, at Ryeyards in Port of Menteith, Lake of Menteith Fisheries (*www.menteithfisheries.co.uk*) offer boat bookings for fly-fishing trips on the 700-acre lake. For details of permits and availability, please contact the Fisheries directly – details are on their website. The Lake of Menteith is the main venue for Scotland's National Fly-Fishing Championships, and access to the lake will vary at different times throughout the year. Additionally, the lake has been named a Site of Special Scientific Interest on account of its outstanding flora and fauna, so it offers much more than being an ideal location for a fishing trip.

Also on the Lake of Menteith, visits to historic Inchmahome Priory (*www.historicenvironment.scot/visit-a-place/places/inchmahome-priory*) by ferry are always popular. This island sanctuary functioned for over three centuries, with Robert the Bruce visiting it three times while King of Scotland. The infant Mary, Queen of Scots was also kept safe at this location during Henry VIII's 'Rough Wooing', when Henry invaded Scotland in the mid-16th century in an attempt to force a marriage between Mary and his son Edward, thus attempting to unite the two kingdoms. Built around 1238, the priory is still renowned for its fine processional doorway and chapter house. Ferries are available between April and September, but it is best to check ahead of time by visiting the website.

Other historical stories in the Aberfoyle area include the legend of the 'Poker Tree', situated close to the main crossroads; while in the village,

don't forget to find out more about this mysterious tree and Baillie Nicol Jarvie, a Glasgow magistrate and cousin of the infamous Rob Roy MacGregor, who once stayed at an inn at the Clachan of Aberfoyle. The tree grows in what had once been the gardens of the Baillie Nicol Jarvie Hotel – now long since converted into residential apartments. The incident refers to a fictional episode from Sir Walter Scott's famous novel *Rob Roy* (1817), where Aberfoyle is used as one of the locations (though named 'Aberfoil') and a red-hot poker allows Jarvie to best a hostile Highlander in combat; the poker was hung from the tree outside the hotel to commemorate the fight. The real Rob Roy MacGregor was himself no stranger to the area, and there are considerable historical accounts relating to his activities there during his lifetime. What is perhaps less well-known is the fact that the village also appeared as the scene of the action in Jules Verne's adventure story *The Child of the Cavern* (1877), an early science fiction tale concerning mysterious subterranean goings-on in a coal mine near Aberfoyle.

Trossachs Pier

Trossachs Pier is situated at the eastern end of splendid Loch Katrine (*www.lochkatrine.com*) in the very heart of the Loch Lomond and the Trossachs National Park, and offers a great family day out in a location unmatched for its magnificent scenery. Trossachs Pier has become famous for its sightseeing cruises on the *Sir Walter Scott* steam-

ship, with one-hour cruises available (though pre-booking is highly recommended), while a two-hour voyage to Stronachlachar on the western shore of Loch Katrine is also available. Checking departure times on the day of your journey is essential; the booking office is conveniently situated at the pier complex, where knowledgeable staff members are on hand to answer enquiries. The website also offers current details of ticket fares, both for the *Sir Walter Scott* and the cruise ship *Lady of the Lake* – the latter named after Scott's famous work which inspired so many visitors to come and see the beauty of the Trossachs for themselves.

The steamship *Sir Walter Scott* has a long and fascinating history of its own, and has become almost as legendary as the celebrated author whose name it bears. Constructed by the Dumbarton-based company of Denny Brothers in 1899, the ship was transported from Dumbarton to Inversnaid upon completion, then conveyed on horse-drawn carriages all the way to Stronachlachar, where it was finally reassembled. Its maiden voyage was in the April of 1900, and the ship remains powered by its original 1898 triple expansion steam engine – though in recognition of a need to move with the times, the engine has used environmentally-friendly biofuel from 2007 onwards.

The *Sir Walter Scott* has received many up-grades to its passenger accommodation over the years, and its range of facilities – along with its painstakingly-maintained period features – mean that it is now regarded as one of the greatest jewels of Scotland's maritime heritage. The ship is popular with walkers, cyclists, families and tourists, and offers full wheelchair access. There is a licensed bar, refreshments and snacks are available, and public toilet facilities are also on board.

The *Sir Walter Scott* can accommodate up to 200 guests, while the *Lady of the Lake* can hold a maximum of 65 visitors. This makes the ships not

only ideal for day trips, but also special events – even including weddings. For details of the many different services that are on offer, including the popular high tea cruises, a visit to the website is highly recommended.

For those who prefer land-based adventures, cycles and electric bikes can be hired from nearby Katrinewheelz (*www.katrinewheelz.co.uk*), a company which allows visitors to explore the historic landscape at their own pace. Trossachs Pier also has a busy and well-stocked gift shop named Katrine Gifts (*www.lochkatrine.com/about/shops-dining*) which offers books, crafts, jewellery and souvenirs for sale as well as food and drink – including local ales and whiskies. There is also a picture window over the glorious Loch Katrine with a view that has to be seen to be believed! Anyone seeking to make a fishing trip on Loch Katrine should consult with Loch Katrine Fisheries (*www.fishlochkatrine.com*), a company which offers a range of fishing services. It is advised to contact them ahead of time for information about fishing seasons, permits, and availability of boats.

Trossachs Pier is also a popular starting point for the much-loved Three Lochs Forest Drive (*www.lochlomond-trossachs.org/things-to-see/lochs-in-the-national-park/three-lochs-forest-drive*); as previously mentioned in the Aberfoyle section, this is a famous seven-mile-long road trip which takes visitors past the magnificent vistas of Lochan Reòidhte, Loch Drunkie and Loch Achray. The drive is especially admired among wildlife enthusi-

asts, as woodland animals and birds can often be seen in their natural habitat. Wild camping and walking trails are also available in and around the area.

Doomsday, a thrilling post-apocalyptic drama directed by Neil Marshall and released in 2008, concerns the effects of a fictional global pandemic on Scotland and featured location filming at Loch Katrine and Doune, as well as nearby Blackness Castle. Additionally, BBC TV's 2008 adaptation of John Buchan's *The 39 Steps*, directed by James Hawes and starring Rupert Penry-Jones in the lead role of Richard Hannay, involved filming in a number of Scottish locations, including Argyll's Lodging in Stirling and Stirling Castle, but perhaps most memorably scenes were included on the steamship *Sir Walter Scott* at Loch Katrine. The loch has similarly been used as a location for *Outlander*'s season 2, and – in appreciation of this fact – *Outlander* cruises have been available from 2019.

Strathyre and Lochearnhead

The villages of Strathyre and Lochearnhead lie within the bounds of the Loch Lomond and the Trossachs National Park. This is a tremendous walking area, with popular destinations including Kirkton Glen in Balquidder, *Beinn an t-sidean* from Strathyre and the Glen Ogle Trail in Lochearnhead. From Strathyre on the Rob Roy Way, visitors can head to Killin in The Highland North section of the Heart 200 route.

Strathyre developed around the arrival of the Callander and Oban Railway in the 1870s, which brought with it a railway station to the village. Since those early days, Strathyre has evolved into a well-known focal point for tourism, with nearby caravan parks, holiday chalets and camp sites for visitors to the region. It is renowned for its walks and cycling routes, and also for its canoeing and watersports activities. Among its many charms is the beautiful Strathyre Forest (*www.visit-*

scotland.com/info/towns-villages/strathyre-forest-p249351), part of the Queen Elizabeth Forest Park, which has been dubbed 'The Sheltered Valley'. The forest is home to many wild animals, including deer and red squirrels, with Forestry Commission signage posted throughout for walkers, hikers and climbers.

Like many other parts of the Trossachs, Strathyre has a literary claim to fame in the fact that poet William Wordsworth and his sister Dorothy visited the village in 1803 and enjoyed walks around its attractive surroundings. His stay would eventually inspire him to write his famous lyric poem *The Solitary Reaper* (1807).

This area also features the astonishing BLiSS Sculpture Trail (*www.seelochlomond.co.uk/discover/bliss-trail*), an acclaimed exhibition of outdoor artwork. The acronym BLiSS stands for the four villages which are linked by the trail: namely Balquidder, Lochearnhead, Strathyre and St Fillans. (The 'I' stands for both Tourist Information and the Innovation in Scotland's Year of Innovation, Architecture and Design, in 2016). BLiSS features a series of art installations which blend into the exquisite scenery, combining creative art with natural beauty. An app for mobile devices, which features an audio tour, has produced as an accompaniment for the trail. On the app, each of the art installations is described either by the artist themselves or a local person native to the area, and there are also photographs and maps to show all of the individual locations in the vicinity.

The nearby village of Lochearnhead has a very long history. Situated on the western end of Loch Earn, this area has been settled for centuries, as recorded by the Neolithic burial chamber at nearby Edinchip, the Druid Field between Kendrum Burn and the Craggan Road, and a Bronze Age lake dwelling (crannog) at the west end of the loch at Carstran Bay. (A separate crannog, Neish Island, can also be found at the eastern end of the loch near St Fillans.) Because Loch Earn was on the frontier between the ancient Scottish lands of Dalriada and Pictland, this border area saw various skirmishes throughout the centuries including the Siege of Dundurn in 683 and the death in battle of King Giric in 889. Scottish folk hero Rob Roy MacGregor lived and died in the region around Loch Voil, and his grave can be found in Balquidder Kirkyard.

Much entertaining mythology and folklore surrounds Lochearnhead, including Chieftains'

Mound – a small hill in the Games Field – which was reputed in olden times to be a faery knoll: home to the *sidhe*. Edinample Castle is said to be haunted by the spirit of its architect, who was reputedly thrown from the roof of the castle in 1630 by its owner, Sir Duncan Campbell of Glenorchy (1550-1631), when the latter – who had a notoriously foul temper – discovered that a parapet had not been built into the stronghold as per his instructions. Other accounts suggest that the grounds upon which the castle would later be built were cursed by Saint Blane many years earlier, back in the 6th century.

Sir Walter Scott's novel *A Legend of Montrose* (1819) drew upon the 'Ardvorlich severed head' incident as its inspiration. This tale relates to Lady Margaret Stewart of Ardvorlich who, while heavily pregnant, gave shelter to a band of MacGregors who visited Ardvorlich House. She did not suspect that the group had recently murdered her brother, John Drummond (of Drummonderinoch, near Comrie), until they placed his severed head on a platter and left it for her to discover. Upon meeting this gruesome sight, Lady Margaret was so distraught that she took flight to the surrounding hills and soon after gave birth to a son, James Baeg Stewart (c.1589-1662), who would later become known as the 'Mad Major of Ardvorlich' – a major player in the later Covenanting Wars. Scott decided to rename Stewart as a fictional character, Allan Macauley, for the events of his novel. The Findlater Sisters, Jane and Mary

Findlater, grew up in Lochearnhead and would go on to produce popular prose fiction – both separately and in collaboration – between 1896 and 1923.

Another legend of the area is that an *each-uisge* (water horse) lives in Loch Earn. (Some variations of the fable suggest that it was expelled from Loch Tay by Fingal.) According to the myth, the horse would lure strangers into attempting to ride on its back, only to drag them down to a watery death. It is thought that this folktale derives from the strong currents which operate within Loch Earn.

Lochearnhead offers more than an illustrious past; today it is a well-regarded tourist destination with a firm emphasis on watersports activities. In particular, it is renowned for its water-skiing, with championship competitions being held on Loch Earn. However, canoeing, kayaking and scuba-diving also regularly take place there. Loch Earn Watersports Centre (*www.lochearnwatersports-centre.com*) is a widely admired venue which offers everything from paddle boarding to wake boarding and many other activities besides.

For those who prefer land activities to those on water, there are two Munros – Ben Vorlich and Stuc a'Chroin – on the Loch Earn side of Lochearnhead, while other popular walking routes include the Glen Ogle trail and the Glen Ample walk. The Balquidder, Lochearnhead and Strathyre Highland Games (*www.lochearnheadhighlandga-mes.co.uk*) take place annually in July, and include

track and field events, heavy events (including caber tossing), and a hill race. Groups planning to organise outdoor activities will want to check out the Hertfordshire Scouts Activity Centre (*www.hertford-shirescouts.org.uk/activity-centres/lochearnhead*), which is based in the old Lochearnhead Railway Station. Now fully restored and converted by its current owners, Hertfordshire Scouts, this activity base provides a perfect place for outdoor pursuits for up to ninety people. The village also hosts a major annual sheep-shearing competition, Lochearnhead Shears, which is now one of the largest contests of its type in the UK.

This area was also used extensively for the production of Ralph Thomas's celebrated 1959 adaptation of John Buchan's novel *The 39 Steps*. Starring Kenneth More as diplomat Richard Hannay, the movie featured location filming at Balquidder, the Falls of Dochart at Killin, Brig o' Turk, Dunblane and Loch Lubnaig.

Chapter Three

The Highland North

FOR outdoor activity enthusiasts and history buffs alike, there is something to suit just about every taste on the Highland North section of Heart 200. From Neolithic stone circles to boat tours and wildlife pastimes, there is no end to the enjoyment for those who are seeking the attractions of the great outdoors. There are also plenty of surprises and unexpected delights in store for anyone who wants to venture into the beauty and tranquillity of the route's stunning Highland North – a place of history and folklore, amazing sights and incredible stories.

Northern Stirlingshire and Highland Perthshire have much more to offer than stunning scenery. This area is steeped in history, and offers many appealing walks and cycle routes for nature enthusiasts. Keep an eye out for the beautiful wildlife around the region, and prepare to encounter many fascinating sights from Scotland's ancient past.

Killin

The beautiful village of Killin is located at the west of Loch Tay, and has many historical claims to fame. It is particularly well-known for the Killin Incident of 1749, when – in the aftershock of the then-recent Jacobite Rising of 1745 – two men wearing Highland tartan in violation of the 1746 Dress Act (which made the wearing of tartan garments illegal) were captured by the British Army for plundering. With the involvement of a mob of local citizens, however, the two men were eventually released by the soldiers. Then, in 1767, the Reverend James Stuart (1701-89) – who was Killin's minister at the time – published the New

Testament of the Bible in Scots Gaelic for the first time. A monument to his memory can be found near the village's Killin Hotel. Killin was also the birthplace of the Reverend Prof. Patrick Campbell MacDougall FRSE (1806-67), who became professor of moral philosophy at Edinburgh University and made many contributions to scholarly life at the time, including becoming the first convenor of the Scottish Free Church's Widows and Orphans Fund.

Killin is situated beside the spectacular Falls of Dochart, an area of great natural beauty where the River Dochart descends at great speed towards Loch Tay. This cascade of waterfalls is spanned by the Bridge of Dochart, constructed in 1760, which offers incredible views of the surging water. The serene island of Inchbuie is situated in the Falls; access is by a small iron gate down a flight of stone steps on the side of the Dochart Bridge at the western end of the island.

Another historical place of interest is Moirlanich Longhouse (*www.nts.org.uk/visit/places/moirlanich-longhouse*) in nearby Glen Lochay, which is maintained by the National Trust for Scotland. A traditional 19th century cruck frame cottage and byre, complete with box beds and a 'hingin' lum', the longhouse remains virtually unchanged since its last inhabitants left the premises in 1968. Now a popular tourist attraction, visitors can enjoy the array of period artefacts on display as well as an unusual feature – layer upon layer of authentic early 20th century wallpaper still in evidence in the house. Opening times are seasonal, so checking the website is advised before your trip.

In the village itself, the Old Mill Killin (*www.killinwatermill.co.uk*) is an historical sight that is well worth viewing. Operated by Killin and

Ardeonaig Trust, the Old Mill is a remarkably-preserved three-storey rubble building thought to date from around 1840, situated near the Bridge of Dochart. Originally used as a meal mill, and then as a tweed mill, its site has been occupied by various different mill buildings over the centuries – the first thought to have

been erected by Christian missionary Saint Fillan in the 8th century. Renovations and maintenance of this noteworthy structure are still ongoing so that it can continue to be enjoyed by future generations.

Killin has an appealing selection of independent shops and places to eat. MacGregor's Market (*www.macgregors.org.uk*) in Main Street offers tourist information as well as local arts and crafts and local produce, while Killin Outdoor Centre and Mountain Shop (*www.killinoutdoor.co.uk*) presents a wide variety of products and services including canoe and kayak hire, as well as maps and guides for walking and cycling. Killin is also the location of a well-attended annual music festival (*www.killinmusicfestival.com*) which features a fantastic line-up of live artists every year.

There are plenty of options for keen walkers around Killin. Popular trails include Loch Tay, Acharn Forest, Sron a'chlachain and Creag Buidhe. Killin railway viaduct commands remarkable views from Loch Tay. The Colin Burt Nature Reserve (*www.visitscotland.com/info/see-do/colin-burt-re-serve-p1159391*) offers an appealing contrast of wet-

land, woodland and river environments, especially for nature lovers hoping to see birds and animals in their natural habitats. Many walkers reach Killin from Strathyre on the Rob Roy Way, heading on to that route's next destination at Ardtainaig. There is also the picturesque Killin Golf Club (*www.killingolfclub.co.uk*) on Aberfeldy Road, widely considered to be one of the most visually attractive 9-hole golf courses in all of Scotland, opened in June 1902 and set within the stunning natural vistas of Highland Perthshire.

History enthusiasts will not want to miss viewing the ancient burial ground of Clan Mac-Nab, which can be found in an enclosure at the end of the island of Inchbuie. Killin has a long history with the MacNab Clan, and the famous Killin Stone Circle (*www.killin.info/guide/kinnell-stone-circle*) – a well-preserved ring of prehistoric stones – can be seen in the private grounds of Kinnell House, the ancient seat of the MacNabs.

In popular culture, Killin's main claim to fame lies with Tomnadashan Mine – a disused copper mine overlooking the village, situated between Killin and Aberfeldy – which is thought to have been the location where the Monty Python's Flying Circus team filmed scenes with the deadly Killer Rabbit of Caerbannog in *Monty Python and the Holy Grail* (1975). The mine was abandoned in 1862 and is quite far off the beaten track, meaning that it is not a recommended destination for inexperienced walkers. While derelict mines are considered hazardous and should only be entered when accompanied by an expert guide, visitors should be advised that the Killer Rabbit itself was blown up by the Holy Hand Grenade of Antioch and is no longer considered a public threat! Glen Lochay, which is located near Killin, was also a destination for Robert Donat's Richard Hannay in Alfred Hitchcock's famous version of *The 39 Steps* (1935).

Kenmore

Situated at the north-east end of the 14-mile-long Loch Tay, where it meets the River Tay, the village of Kenmore dates back to the 16th century. Originally known as 'Balloch' when founded by Sir Colin Campbell of Glenorchy (1512-83) in 1540, the village was later moved to the opposite side of the River Tay and its current configuration owes its form to the layout of the 3rd Earl of Breadalbane who restructured Kenmore as a model village in 1760. Balloch Castle, built by Campbell in 1550, was succeeded by the grand neo-Gothic Taymouth

Castle, built on the same site. When approaching the village from Killin, visitors are welcomed by the huge, imposing archway at the gateway to Taymouth Castle Estate. This beautiful location is where Queen Victoria spent part of her honeymoon with Prince Albert in 1842. At time of writing, the castle is closed and undergoing renovation, so it is not currently accessible to the public. *Mrs Brown*, Jeremy Brock's Oscar-nominated historical drama from 1997, starring Judi Dench as Queen Victoria and Sir Billy Connolly as her ghillie John Brown, included scenes filmed at Taymouth Castle which doubled for Balmoral Castle.

Kenmore has a long and illustrious history, as can be witnessed by the nearby Croft Moraig Stone Circle (*www.britainexpress.com/Scotland/Tayside/ancient/croft-moraig.htm*), situated near the A827 between Kenmore and Aberfeldy. This complex multi-phase historical site was excavated in 1965, and thought to have originated some 5,000 years ago. Archaeologists have uncovered pottery fragments from the site which are thought to date to around 2000 BC. Around a mile and a half beyond the end of Acharn Falls, near Kenmore, is the Greenland Stone Circle (*www.inspirock.com/united-kingdom/kenmore/greenland-stone-circle-a7-470428525*), a site which contains informational notices explaining its intriguing historical details – as well as providing many beautiful views on the journey.

Another interesting historical site for visitors to the area is the Kenmore Hotel (*www.kenmorehotel.com*), which was commissioned by the village's original laird, Sir Colin Campbell, in 1572. However, it is thought to have been built around an existing tavern on the same site which had been constructed some 70 years beforehand, meaning that the current building is considered by many to be the oldest hotel in all of Scotland. It is still serving customers today.

In recent years, Kenmore has become a very popular destination for watersports. Taymouth Marina Watersports (*www.taymouthmarina.com*) offers a comprehensive array of aquatic activities and equipment hire including paddle boards, inflatables, pedalos, motor fishing boats, kayaks, canoes and much more besides. Loch Tay Boating Centre (*www.loch-tay.co.uk*) is also well worth your attention, specialising in fishing and small cruise boats but also offering numerous other maritime services besides.

Informative and entertaining tours on the loch are also available from Loch Tay Safaris (*www.lochtaysafaris.net*), where visitors can learn about the rich past and present of the area including the history and folklore of the loch itself – one of the deepest in Scotland. With fascinating facts about this notable place and its heritage, visitors are guaranteed to learn something new about this extraordinary part of the world.

History aficionados should also be aware of the Isle of Loch Tay (*www.canmore.org.uk/site/24932/loch-tay-priory-island*), the largest island in the loch, which is known in Gaelic as *Eilean nam Bannaomh* – 'The Isle of Holy Women'. As its name suggests, the island was the site of a nunnery in the 12th century, though a castle was built there many years later in the 14th century as the residence of the Earl of Strathearn. It is noted as the final resting place of Sibylla of Normandy (1092-1122), the wife of King Alexander I (c.1078-1124) who reigned over Scotland from 1107 until 1124.

Visitors interested in cultural heritage will surely be keen for a trip to the Scottish Crannog Centre (*www.crannog.co.uk*), which offers guided tours of a reconstructed Iron Age loch-dwelling. The museum features history exhibitions hosted by a knowledgeable staff, with many crafts and music demonstrations taking place on various dates. The crannog is a highly accurate, full-size reconstruction

of an artificial island as it would have looked in its day, and is closely based on the findings at the Oakbank crannog site. Numerous artefacts from excavations throughout the area are on display at the visitor centre, and the staff members take historical precision very seriously in order to provide the best possible visitor experience. The museum is dedicated to bringing history alive, and among the many experiences that visitors can encounter there are Iron Age recipes made with the very same ingredients that crannog-dwellers would have used, an example of 2500-year-old butter on display, and accurate aromas from the outdoor areas – including that of an ancient wood fire, setting the scene perfectly. Demonstrations are given on how to make fire using a bow and wood, and visitors also have the opportunity to dress up as a villager from the period – or perhaps even a chieftain! A visit to their website for information about admissions fees and opening hours is highly recommended.

Arts and crafts enthusiasts are sure to enjoy a visit to Karelia House (*www.kareliahouse.co.uk*) near Comrie Bridge in Kenmore, which offers an amazing selection of craft supplies and is considered to be one of Scotland's premier craft destinations. With yarns, fabrics, patterns and sewing machines on sale, along with crafting materials, Karelia House also offers many craft courses suitable for a wide range of skill levels, including instruction in

dressmaking, knitting and crochet, patchwork, sewing, textiles and machine embroidery. Retreats are also sometimes on offer, so be sure to check their website for dates and availability. And if all that wasn't enough, they also offer a cosy café area with snacks and drinks to suit just about every taste.

For pony trekking, the Mains of Taymouth Stables (*www.taymouth.co.uk/on-site-facilities/stables.php*) are situated within the Mains of Taymouth Country Estate and offer horse-riding experiences around beautiful woodland areas under the supervision of trained staff. For golfers, Mains of Taymouth Golf Course (*www.taymouth.co.uk/on-site-facilities/kenmore-golf-course.php*) offers a pleasant and challenging golf experience in astonish-

ingly beautiful parkland scenery, which has led to the course frequently being dubbed 'Perthshire's finest nine holes'. For those who prefer walking, following the Drummond Hill Walk will take visitors to the stunning panorama of one of Kenmore's most celebrated scenic spots, Black Rock viewpoint (*www.walkhighlands.co.uk/Perthshire/drummond-hill.shtml*).

Aberfeldy

The historical market town of Aberfeldy has no shortage of attractions for the Heart 200 visitor. Located in Strath Tay, the town is popular with walkers and hikers due to its proximity to many popular peaks including Ben Lawers, Creag Odhar, Sron Mhor and Farragon Hill. Aberfeldy was granted Fairtrade Town status in 2002.

The town has become instantly recognisable thanks to its association with Robert Burns's famous 1787 poem *The Birks of Aberfeldy*. There is

now a one-and-a-half mile walking trail around the Birks (*www.walkhighlands.co.uk/perthshire/birks-of-aberfeldy.shtml*) – a beautiful valley which no countryside wanderer will want to pass up the chance of experiencing for themselves. While admiring this scenic walk, visitors will want to keep a lookout for a monument to Burns's poem which commemorates the work of Scotland's national

bard while also inviting everyone to admire the beauty of this tranquil area during their stay in the town. This gorge of the Moness Burn has also been named a Site of Special Scientific Interest due to the wide range of its flora and fauna.

Aberfeldy is also especially well-known for its Tay Bridge, a William Adam-designed 'Wade's Bridge' constructed in 1733 affording striking views of the town and considered by General George Wade himself to be among his greatest accomplishments. On the banks of the River Tay, in a park overlooking the bridge, can be found the commanding and moving Black Watch Monument (*www.britainexpress.com/scotland/Tayside/properties/black-watch-memorial-aberfeldy.htm*): a famous statue of a lone soldier standing high upon a cairn, which commemorates the service and sacrifices of the Black Watch battalions.

Visitors seeking to know more about the area's history will also be keen to visit the nearby Castle Menzies (*www.castlemenzies.org*), a 16th century castle that was once occupied by the forces of Oliver Cromwell. It would later be seized by Jacobites in 1715, and then played host to Bonnie Prince Charlie in 1746 when he was on his way to the Battle of Culloden. While the castle's historical significance is of great interest to visitors, equally fascinating has been its painstaking restoration by the Menzies Clan Society; this has meant that the original structure of the building remains sound and can be enjoyed by visitors today. The castle is now maintained by the Menzies Charitable Trust.

Animal lovers will enjoy a trip to Cluny House Gardens (*www.clunyhousegardens.com*), a beautiful woodland garden which has become especially famed for the red squirrel population on the site. The garden was created by Bob and Betty Masterton in the 1950s, and over the decades it has been gradually developed to include some wonderful features including unusual varieties of tree, and rare Himalayan plants. Since 1987 the gardens have been maintained by Wendy Mattingley, daughter of the original owners, and her husband John Mattingley. In addition to the amazing array of horticultural delights on display, Cluny House Gardens are also home to a wonderful assortment of wild birds, making them the perfect destination for all wildlife lovers.

Nearby Errichel House and Restaurant (*www.errichelhouseandrestaurant.co.uk*) is also a popular place for visitors due to the long-held dedication of its staff to care for and preserve rare breeds of farm animal. These include Toggenburg goats, Shetland sheep and cattle, Highland ponies, and a duck pond containing Mallards, Cayuga, Khaki Ducks, and other poultry breeds including geese. Visitors may also want to enquire about the guided farm walks, offering stunning views around the beautiful Perthshire countryside.

Top destinations for walkers around Aberfeldy include St David's Well along the Weem Forest Trail (*www.britainexpress.com/scotland/Tayside/countryside/weem-forest.htm*), an ancient holy well situated at the Rock of Weem thought to date back to the 7th century, which has historical links to St Cuthbert. The delightful Bolfracks Gardens on the picturesque banks of the River Tay (*www.bolfracks.com*) have also become one of the area's most beloved attractions. The gardens date back until at least the 18th century, and contain an impressive selection of rare horticultural specimens. Though the estate is privately owned, the gardens can be accessed by the public between April and October; for details of admissions fees, please visit their website.

One of Aberfeldy's top tourist destinations is the celebrated Dewar's Aberfeldy Distillery (*www.dewars.com/gl/en/aberfeldydistillery*), a company that has become virtually synonymous with the town due to the high regard with which their product is held. The distillery features a whisky lounge, café, and plenty of information about Scotland's most famous alcoholic beverage including an interactive exhibition. Especially fa-

mous for its Aberfeldy single malt Scotch whisky, the distillery was founded in 1896 as John Dewar and Sons Ltd., with the building officially opening in 1898. The distillery was extended in 1972, and in 2000 the 'Dewar's World of Whisky' centre was formally opened by the Earl of Elgin. This new installation was designed to provide information to the public about the whisky distillation process and the fascinating history of the Dewar's company.

The outstandingly preserved Monzie Castle (*www.monzieestate.com*), on the Monzie Estate near Aberfeldy, is an historic building which initially dates from 1634, though its current form is due to works completed by architect John Paterson (?-1832) between 1785 and 1790. This beautiful castle, which stands in impressive grounds, can be visited by the public only during select times of the year; check their website for details of when the building can be accessed for tours, as well as information about admission charges.

For younger visitors to Aberfeldy, there is Victoria Park (*www.pkc.gov.uk/article/15319/Victoria-Park-in-Aberfeldy*) – the largest and most popular public park in the town – which features play areas including a skate park, a vintage steam road-roller, swings, slides, grassy spaces for ball games, and picnic benches. The town also features a nine-hole golf course, Aberfeldy Golf Club (*www.aberfeldy-golfclub.co.uk*), which was founded in 1895 and is situated amidst stunning parkland scenery. The club also presents a unique feature in that the Aberfeldy Footbridge – which spans the River Tay, and was built entirely of composite materials – famously connects two holes of the golf course which are divided by the river. For anyone seeking more strenuous outdoor activities, Beyond Adventure (*www.beyondadventure.co.uk*) is a specialist outdoor company offering the very best experiences of Perthshire's rural environment. Amongst the wilderness activities they offer are open canoeing, hiking, kayaking and paddle-boarding, though many other services are provided such as skills courses and expeditions.

There is also much to offer the arts enthusiast in Aberfeldy, not least the famous Birks Cinema (*www.birkscinema.co.uk*) right at the heart of the town. Originally operating between the 1930s and 1980s, the cinema's interior was converted into an amusement hall until it was closed in 2004. However, the Friends of the Birks organisation bought the building in 2009 with funding from the Scottish Government Town Centre Regeneration

Fund, and after further capital had been sourced the cinema was fully refurbished, reopening in 2013 with a modern 92-seat auditorium and café bar. The project's patron was award-winning actor Alan Cumming, who was born in Aberfeldy. The cinema continues to screen the latest film releases, and remains a well-attended venue.

On the subject of movies, Hugh Hudson's multiple Academy Award-winning 1981 biopic *Chariots of Fire* featured a recreation of the Highland Games which was filmed in the Sma' Glen at Aberfeldy, where Ian Charleson (in the role of Olympic Gold Medallist Eric Liddell) can be seen awarding prizes to participants. Aberfeldy has another unusual claim to fame in popular culture, in that it has a musical band named after it; formed in Edinburgh in 2002, singer-songwriter Riley Briggs decided to name his group Aberfeldy due to the fact that his grandfather once had a caravan in the town and visited it regularly.

Fortingall

A beautiful village which features some outstanding thatched cottages and plenty of rural charm, Fortingall has been home to some momentous history in its lifetime. Its name derives from the Gaelic *Fairtairchill* (literally, 'the church below an escarpment'), and has a long history as a settlement. In particular, after an article on the subject was published in *The New York Times* in 1899 it has been claimed that Roman Prefect Pontius Pilate was born in Fortingall and spent his childhood in the village. Pilate lived from around 20BC to some point after 36AD, and was the Prefect of the Roman Judea from 26AD to 36AD. (In reality Pilate is known to have been born some decades before the Romans invaded Britain under the reign of Emperor Claudius in 43AD, and his Biblical role would have taken place long prior to Roman troops reaching Scotland.)

The village's long history is reflected in the large number of Neolithic sites in its vicinity. Its prehistoric significance has been of huge interest to archaeologists over the years, with many excavations taking place in the area. A standing stone known as *Carn-na-Marbh* (the 'cairn of the dead') (*www.canmore.org.uk/site/24996/ carn-na-marbh*) is situated near the village and dates back to the 14th century when the settlement was all but wiped out from the Black Death; the stone is situated atop a reused tumulus (a burial mound) originally thought to date back to the Bronze Age, and believed to mark the site of the mass grave that the villagers were buried in by the only survivor of the plague. There are many other such ancient sites of interest to be found around the village, not least its admired Stone Circles (*www.thehazeltree.co.uk/2014/05/11/the-stone-circles-of-fortingall/*).

The village of Fortingall was remodelled and rebuilt by shipping magnate and Member of Parliament Sir Donald Currie (1825-1909) in the early 1890s, based upon designs of architect James MacLaren (1853-90), who also designed Stirling High School (now the Stirling Highland Hotel). Currie's plans would see the Fortingall's buildings, including the church, being remodelled in the Scottish vernacular style which later inspired internationally-acclaimed architect and designer Charles Rennie Mackintosh (1868-1928). Among the village's most prominent architectural features is the Fortingall Hotel (*www.fortingall.com*), which is a noteworthy example of Scottish vernacular revival. The original hotel (which had been a combination

of Victorian and 17th century rural construction) was torn down, and the current building's crow-stepped gables and burgh architecture bear the inspiration of both Lowland Scottish and English influences. Today, this elegant four-star hotel offers rooms with country or garden views, a restaurant and bar area, and all modern conveniences. It is particularly popular with people planning to explore the many walks around this peaceful area, and its famous visitors have included cricketer Andrew 'Freddie' Flintoff.

Fortingall Parish Church (*www.scotlandschurchestrust.org.uk/church/fortingall-parish-church/*) is built on an early Christian site, thought to be founded around 700AD by Bishop Coeddi of Iona as a 'daughter' monastery; the 'Arts and Crafts' style of the current church building was intended to harmonise with the rest of the village when it was remodelled in 1900-02 according to the designs of W. Dunn and R. Watson. The earlier,

18th century church's belfry can still be seen in an enclosure near the current building. The churchyard is also the site of a Commonwealth Memorial Cemetery, under the auspices of the Commonwealth War Graves Commission (*www.cwgc.org/find-a-cemetery/2079157/Fortingall%20Parish%20Churchyard*).

The churchyard's most famous feature is the Fortingall Yew (*www.visitscotland.com/info/towns-villages/fortingall-yew-p249411*), now protected by a walled enclosure. The tree is considered to be between 3000 and 9000 years of age, and thought to be one of the oldest living things in all of Europe. The Fortingall Yew is believed to have been an ancient giant at the beginning of recorded history, and at its peak it boasted a breadth of 56 feet (just over 17 metres). Its branches now overhang the final resting place of the Stewarts of Garth, who were the descendants of the third son of King Robert II: Alexander Stewart (1343-1405),

Earl of Buchan, better known as the infamous Wolf of Badenoch.

Situated between Fortingall and Aberfeldy, the acclaimed Highland Safaris and Red Deer Centre (*www.highlandsafaris.net*) is an award-winning nature experience that no visitor will want to miss out on seeing for themselves. The company offers a variety of safari experiences including a mountain safari, forest safari, biking safaris, walking safaris, and various other services such as 4x4 off-road driving, seasonal safari experiences, and gold and gem panning. It is recommended that visitors check their website ahead of time to be sure of the full range and availability of activities at the time of their trip. Other much-loved pursuits on site include the red deer barn – where guests can learn more about these wonderful animals before meeting the resident tame herd – and encountering the company's very own barn owl, where this amazing nocturnal avian can be seen up close under the supervision of an expert handler.

Fortingall also has some little-known pop culture renown in that its charming natural surroundings meant that it was once considered potentially the ideal filming location for Vincente Minnelli's famed 1954 MGM musical *Brigadoon*. Director Minnelli and star Gene Kelly were both eager to film in Scotland, but the high production costs and unreliability of the weather (to say nothing of the midges!) meant that the movie was eventually produced on MGM's sound stages in the United States instead.

Kinloch Rannoch and Tummel Bridge

At the eastern end of Loch Rannoch and on the banks of the River Tummel, the village of Kinloch Rannoch (*www.kinlochrannoch.com*) is one of the most amazingly scenic locations in Highland Perthshire – and, some would say, in Scotland as a whole.

Though the settlement existed for centuries as a remote hamlet due to its advantageous geographical location, its place in history was cemented by the role it played in the Jacobite risings; Rannoch's clans played an active part in the conflict, and the Rannoch estates were commandeered from their chieftains by the Crown following Battle of Culloden in 1746. Under the supervision of James Small (1725-77), a former Ensign in Lord Loudoun's Regiment who was appointed factor of the Robertson of Struan estates near Kinloch Rannoch, the village was considerably enlarged and developed. Before his arrival, there were no roads in the area and starvation had become common. Small moved quickly to ensure that former soldiers received support to become crofters, oversaw the construction of roads, bridges and schools, and made an attempt to drain the surrounding marshlands and thus provide more fertile agricultural ground.

Today, Kinloch Rannoch has become a well-known tourist area due to its focus on outdoor activities, while it has also become a popular site for agriculture, hydroelectric power generation and forestry. Among its many visual attractions are its Old Bridge over the Tummel, which dates to 1764, and the beautiful waterfall on the Allt Mor burn, situated on the approach to the village. One of the area's most famous walks takes visitors to Craig Var, a rocky crag which overlooks the valley and offers an incredible view not just of Kinloch Rannoch, but all of the surrounding area. The village also has an unusual feature in the form of the 'Sleeping Giant' – a hill which resembles the head, shoulders and chest of a huge man. Local legend suggests that the giant will one day awaken from his slumber, but only when he hears particular notes being played from his master's flute.

The perfect introduction to the area, and historic Rannoch Moor in particular, can be found at Rannoch Moor Visitor Centre (*www.britainexpress.com/attractions.htm?attraction=1331*), a heritage showcase which is based in the buildings of Rannoch Station. The station dates back to the railway originally built between Glasgow and Fort William (and later extended as far as Mallaig).

Construction on the tracks began in 1889, and the line across Rannoch Moor was completed in 1894. The extraordinary history of the West Highland Line is retold in the visitor centre, along with fascinating details of the area's complex geography and information about the many walking and cycling routes. The station has also become famous for its perennially popular Rannoch Station Tea Room (*www.rannochstationtearoom.co.uk*), which the owners proudly state is the most remote tearoom in all of Scotland. At the heart of Rannoch Moor,

based on Rannoch Station platform, the tearoom offers home cooking from the finest local produce, and is open from March to October every year.

Visiting artists and crafters will no doubt find much to impress them at the Shed Gallery (*www.rannochshed.co.uk*), a photographic gallery and graphic design service based at the Old Smiddy in Kinloch Rannoch Square. It is owned by acclaimed photographer Ian Biggs. For those seeking adventure in the great outdoors, Highland Exploration (*www.highlandexploration.com*), based at Rannoch Lodge, offers personally-crafted tours of the area via Land Rover safaris and boat tours. Contacting the company ahead of time to book your outdoor experience is highly recommended, as they offer many additional services including fishing and field crafts.

The prominent All Saints Episcopal Church (*www.rannochandtummel.co.uk/directory-All-Saints-Episcopal-Church-id45*) in Kinloch Rannoch features an 1875 memorial obelisk on its grounds to commemorate the life of Dugald Buchanan (1716-68) – a schoolmaster and poet native to the area. Buchanan's poetry was written both in English and Scots Gaelic, and he is credited as having assisted Killin's Rev. James Stuart in translating the Bible's New Testament into Gaelic for the first time.

Kinloch Rannoch was one of the locations used in *Outlander*'s season 1, where the characters of Claire and Frank enjoy their second honeymoon following the conclusion of World War II. The mystic stone circles at Craigh na Dun enable Claire

(Caitriona Balfe) to travel between 1945 and 1743. On account of the incredibly picturesque scenery in the area, Kinloch Rannoch has been a popular location for film production, with features shot in the area having included Bob Keen's drama *Shepherd on the Rock* (1993), Robbie Moffat's mystery thriller *Finding Fortune* (2003) and Garry Gallon's tense short film *The Rural Theory* (2006).

Between Loch Rannoch and Loch Tummel, the 1,083 metre (3,553 feet) tall mountain Schiehallion is arguably the most famous peak in Perthshire. Its name is thought to be an anglicised variation on the Gaelic name *Sidh Chailleann*, meaning 'Mound of the Caledonians', and Schiehallion is often known as 'the Centre of Scotland' – though of course, the exact geographical centre-point of the country is hotly disputed by cartographers and geographers! The mountain's slopes have been inhabited and cultivated for centuries, starting at least as early as the first millennium BC, and it is host to a rich ecosystem of botanical life which has made it an area of special interest to conservationists. As a Munro, it is a popular destination for hillwalkers, and a new path to the summit was constructed by the John Muir Trust after they purchased the estate in 1999. From the apex of Schiehallion, Scotland's tallest mountain – Ben Nevis – can be seen on a clear day. The peak is also famous for having been the location of the 'Schiehallion Experiment' in 1774, when astronomer Charles Mason (1728-86), forever remembered for his part in surveying the American Mason-Dixon Line between Mary-

land and Pennsylvania, selected it for a revolutionary scientific investigation. He sought to prove that deflecting a pendulum by the mass of the mountain would provide an estimate of the Earth's mean density, meaning that the planet's mass could be deduced along with a value of the gravitational constant that had been postulated by Sir Isaac Newton (1642-1727). Newton had rejected the experiment as a practical demonstration of his theory, and Mason later declined a commission to enact the test, so it eventually fell to the Astronomer Royal, the Rev Dr Nevil Maskelyne, FRS, FRSE (1765-1811), to lead a team to conduct the experiment.

Schiehallion has been a prominent fixture in Scottish popular culture, especially in song. Folk band Gaberlunzie released a track named '(The Back of) Schiehallion' (2002), while power metal band Gloryhammer features the mountain in the lyrics of their song 'The Fires of Ancient Cosmic Destiny' (2019). Traditional country dance 'The

Schiehallion Reel' is named for the mountain, as is the song 'Schiehallion' produced by rock band King Rizla for their album *Time for a New Day* (1994). The march 'Schiehallion', composed by Donald Shaw Ramsay, has featured as the signature tune of Schiehallion Pipes and Drums. The mountain also featured as the location of the climax to Grant Morrison's comic book serial *Zenith* (1987), and Clackmannanshire's Harviestoun Brewery produce a Schiehallion cask-conditioned lager. There is even a Schiehallion Oilfield, situated west of Shetland, which is named in honour of the mountain.

The attractive village of Tummel Bridge is situated at the head of Loch Tummel, where the old bridge crosses the River Tummel. There are two bridges over the Tummel at Tummel Bridge; the eldest was built in 1734 by General George Wade and is now pedestrianised, while the most recent carries traffic from nearby Aberfeldy along the B846. Tummel Bridge is of great archaeological interest due to the large number of duns, stone circles and fort ruins in the area, not least the arresting Na Clachan Aoraidh standing stone circle (*www.canmore.org.uk/site/25877/na-clachan-aoraidh*) in the Allean Forest, which dates from the Bronze Age. There are also several listed buildings in the village, including one of Scotland's first hydroelectric power stations, Tummel Hydroelectric Station (*sse.com/whatwedo/ourprojectsandassets/renewables/tummel/*), built in 1935. The building contains two generating sets with a total capacity of 34MW, and is part of the Tummel Valley hydroelectric scheme. Near the village is the privately-owned mansion Fincastle House (*www.scottishplaces.info/features/featurefirst4907.html*), a grand 17th century structure with historical links to the Stewart family which was once the seat of Sir Robert Gilmour Colquhoun (1803-70), British Consul General in Egypt. Today it is owned by the Barbour Family of Bonskeid.

Situated between Tummel Bridge and Pitlochry, four miles west of the Garry Bridge, the famous Queen's View and Visitors Centre (*www.visitscotland.com/info/towns-villages/queens-view-p402191*) overlooks Loch Tummel, and is one of the most iconic vantage points in the country. The view from the Queen's View offers a breathtaking sight of this area of natural beauty in all of its splendour, while the visitor's centre presents considerable information about the surrounding region. With its regal name, many believe the viewpoint to have been named after Queen Victoria, who visited it in 1866. However, others consider that its stately title may date much further back in time, with its origins possibly having derived

from Queen Isabella of Scotland, wife of King Robert the Bruce.

The Tummel Bridge area is home to the expansive Loch Tummel National Scenic Area (*www.natureflip.com/places/loch-tummel-national-scenic-area*), and has become very popular with walkers, campers and anglers (with fishing managed by the Loch Rannoch Conservation Association, which is responsible for issuing permits). The well-regarded Loch Tummel Sailing Club (*www.lochtummelsc.org*) is situated at Foss, on the loch's south-west shore, and its wide variety of events and services are sure to delight marine enthusiasts. Family-friendly outdoor experiences include dinghy and keelboat sailing between April and September, with training and social events also available. The club is especially well-known for Tummel Week, where a series of races takes place over the course of a week and dozens of boats are hosted for the event.

Bruar and Blair Atholl

Foremost amongst the natural features of the village of Bruar is the celebrated sight of the Falls of Bruar (*www.walkhighlands.co.uk/perthshire/falls-of-bruar.shtml*), a beautiful waterfall in forest surroundings which is just a short two-mile walk away from the heart of the village. There are two walking routes, each leading to two different waterfalls depending on how far visitors want to trek. Geologists believe the falls were formed after the retreat of glaciers from the last Ice Age, at some point dur-

ing the last 10,000 years, and the total drop from the falls is around 60 metres. The Falls of Bruar became famous as a tourist attraction at the end of the 18th century, though at that point the surrounding landscape was devoid of trees and thus relatively bleak. Upon visiting the falls, Robert Burns felt compelled to write a poem, *The Humble Petition of Bruar Water (to the Noble Duke of Athole)*, in 1787, where – in the whimsical guise of the waterfalls themselves – he implored the landowner, the 4th Duke of Atholl, to increase the flora around the area to increase its aesthetic value. In 1796, after Burns had died, the Duke – John Murray KT, PC, FRS (1755-1830) – assented to the request of Scotland's national bard and planted some 120,000 Larch and Scots Pine trees, along with the two bridges which overlook the falls and the path from the village which remains in use until this day.

Always popular with shoppers is the House of Bruar (*www.houseofbruar.com*), considered one of Britain's foremost Scottish country clothing specialists. However, clothing is not all that is on sale

in this extensive complex; customers are also invited to browse the gallery of artworks, consider the large array of gifts and fishing supplies on sale in the store, pay a visit to the food hall, and enjoy the restaurant and conservatory area.

The House of Bruar is generally considered among the most prestigious independent stores in all of Scotland, and its award-winning delicatessen and butchery have become highly sought-after destinations for visitors to the much-admired food hall. Its knitwear department is thought to contain the largest collection of Cashmere products in the entire United Kingdom at time of writing, and there are many other garments on display including numerous varieties of tweed.

For those seeking gifts to reflect their stay in Scotland, the country living and present shop contains a variety of departments which present gift ideas suitable for any taste. It is also the perfect destination for home decoration or ornamentation.

Those seeking to peruse the art gallery will similarly find an extensive range of work from many new and established artists, with subject matter often reflecting the nature and scenery of Scotland.

Bruar is also home to the Clan Donnachaidh Centre and Museum (*www.blairatholl.org.uk/ things-to-see-do/history-and-heritage/Clan-Donna- chaidh-Centre.htm*), situated near the House of Bruar complex. Built in 1969, it is the first custom-built clan museum in Scotland, and in addition to its wealth of information about the Clan Donnachaidh the building hosts a well-stocked gift shop featuring a variety of themed souvenirs – many of which bear clan names and crests.

Just over three miles to the east of Bruar is historic Blair Atholl. An important town, founded where the River Tilt and River Garry converge, Blair Atholl is now included in the Cairngorms National Park and offers plenty to enjoy for the history aficionado in particular. The main road

between Inverness and Perth ran through Blair Atholl until 1984, at which point it was bypassed by the A9. The town, as it stands today, developed around the parish church in the early 19th century when it was relocated from the village of Old Blair.

The oldest building in Blair Atholl town is considered to be the charming Old Watermill (*www.blairathollwatermill.com*), a working watermill which dates back to the 1590s. The building is still used to mill oatmeal and flours, and these are on sale to the public. In addition to the mill shop, the building is also now home to a popular tea room. The Watermill also features a museum, which is open during the summer months. Please check their website for times and availability.

The informative and engaging Atholl Country Life Museum (*www.blairatholl.org.uk/things-to-see-do/visattractions/Atholl-Country-Life-Museum.html*), situated conveniently near the local caravan park, also provides an enlightening and educational experience with many exhibits which outline Scotland's cultural and social history. Among the displays that are available for public viewing are an authentically-recreated 1930s Post Office, the town doctor's horse sleigh, a period kitchen (complete with box bed), and artefacts from the town's old school, church and 'smiddy' (blacksmith's shop).

Those who prefer the outdoor life will enjoy the walking routes around the picturesque and peaceful Glen Tilt (*www.walkhighlands.co.uk/perthshire/glen-tilt.shtml*), a scenic glen near Blair Atholl which offers visitors a number of different trails from the gentle to the more challenging. Cycling trips and advice on various routes around the area are available from nearby Blair Atholl Bike Hire (*www.blairathollbikehire.co.uk*). Also of keen interest to sightseers will be Blair Atholl's famous railway station, on Tulloch Road, which was opened by the Inverness and Perth Junction Railway in 1863 and is still in operation today.

Blair Atholl's most prominent feature, Blair Castle (*www.blair-castle.co.uk*), is now one of the best-regarded stately homes in Scotland, and holds the distinction of having been the last castle in British history to face a siege (in 1746, during the last Jacobite Uprising). The historic seat of the Earls and Dukes of Atholl, the castle is a Category A listed building and occupies a commanding position in Glen Garry. Building on the site is thought to have been commenced by John Comyn, Lord of Badenoch (c.1215-75) in 1269, and has a long and fascinating history which winds through the centuries. After John Murray was named Earl of Atholl in 1629, Blair Castle has remained in the hands of the Murray family – though it was temporarily occupied by Oliver Cromwell's invading army in 1650 and the Jacobite Army in the 18th century. Queen Victoria and Prince Albert visited Blair Castle in 1844, and stayed there for a time. Following her visit, Victoria gave Royal assent to the creation of the famous Atholl Highlanders Regiment. Blair Castle now includes the garrison for the Atholl Highlanders, who are widely recognised as the only legal private army in all of Europe.

Thirty-two of Blair Castle's rooms are open to the public as part of guided tours which illustrate the building's history and its highly significant collections of artwork, fine furniture, historical artefacts and hunting trophies, amongst many other features. Tour guides will explain the complex architecture of the castle, which has been greatly expanded over the century. The oldest section of the building, Comyn's Tower, stands six storeys high and is thought to retain some material from the 13th century, while many of the castle's most famous features date from remodelling by 19th century architects. Artefacts from the castle's long history are on display, including Jacobite relics and even weapons that were used at the Battle of Culloden.

The Atholl Estates contain the historic burial ground of the Dukes of Atholl, which is situated close to the ruins of St Bride's Kirk (once the church of the village of Old Blair). The expansive

grounds comprise a great many fascinating features including the nine-acre walled Hercules Garden, which was restored back to its original Georgian design in 1996. Other sites of interest include a Gothic folly, a red deer park and the remarkable Diana's Grove: a collection of some of the country's finest tree specimens, it is a true horticulturist's delight. The grove is home to a Grand Fir tree which – its height having been measured at 62.7 metres (206 feet) in 2009 – was officially recognised as Britain's second-tallest tree.

Blair Castle is also the location of an extensive gift shop, which offers items inspired by the castle's collections including tartans as well as food and drink. Then there is the award-winning Tullibardine Restaurant, which offers everything from afternoon teas to three-course lunches. Many activities take place on the estate grounds, including a tractor and trailer tour, pony trekking, off-road safaris for native wildlife devotees, and over 40 miles of marked trails for anyone who enjoys ex-

ploring on foot or by bike. Guests are encouraged to visit the Blair Atholl Information Centre in the town for details of the full range of services that are available. Blair Castle is open to the public between March and October, so visitors should check the website for up-to-date details of opening times and admission costs.

Atholl Estates have another claim to fame in the form of Blair Atholl Jamborette, which has taken place in the grounds of Blair Castle every two years since 1946. This is the largest regular Scout camp in Scotland, where well over a thousand Scouts from many countries across the world converge on Blair Atholl to take part in a range of events.

ITV's sumptuous historical drama *Victoria*, starring Jenna Coleman in the lead role of the titular monarch since its inception in 2016, has presented scenes filmed around Blair Atholl, including Blair Castle (specifically, in the 2017 episode 'The King Over the Water'). The castle and surrounding Atholl Estates also appeared in STV's *Con-*

quer the Castle (2008), a reality TV show presented by Alison Craig.

Killiecrankie

A historic village on the banks of the River Garry, Killiecrankie (from the Gaelic *Coille Chreithnich*, meaning 'aspen wood') is famed for being the site of the eponymous Battle of Killiecrankie in 1689, which took place between the Jacobites and the government forces of King William III. The village has become immortalised by the folk song *The Braes of Killiecrankie* (with lyrics attributed to none other than Robert Burns) – perhaps most famously performed by The Corries in their innovative 1966 music video – and has since been the location of the BBC's music series *The Highland Sessions* (2010), presented by Mary Ann Kennedy.

Killiecrankie is an area of outstanding natural beauty, and the village features a footbridge and various viewpoints with commanding sights of the area's awe-inspiring landscape. Near the main settlement is a Roman fortified mound and ditch which was part of the historic Gask Ridge (*www.castlesfortsbattles.co.uk/m/gask_ridge_frontier.html*) – older than both Hadrian's Wall and the Antonine Wall – which also includes the nearby ruins of signal towers used by the Romans to warn of approaching Picts.

A National Trust for Scotland Visitor Centre (*www.nts.org.uk/visit/places/Killiecrankie*) is available at Killiecrankie, which gives plenty of information about the Pass of Killiecrankie and the history of the village. Tales from the past include that of the famous 'Soldier's Leap' – the point where Redcoat soldier Donald McBane (or MacBean) is said to have cleared the Pass of Killiecrankie in a single bound (a distance of approximately 5.5 metres, or 18 feet, across the River Garry) when retreating from the Battle of Killiecrankie, avoiding capture. A Memorial Field to soldiers killed in action during the battle is situated in the grounds of Urrard House, a listed building near the village.

For those seeking a modern-day adrenaline rush, Highland Fling Bungee at the Killiecrankie Bungee Centre (*www.bungeejumpscotland.co.uk*) offers the chance for participants to see this striking village from a slightly different perspective as they leap from a jump platform on the Garry Bridge for a forty metre freefall experience before returning safely to terra firma, all under the watchful management of experienced bungee supervisors. Highland Fling has become famous throughout the country, and so far have held no less than three weddings on their bungee platform, the first having taken place in 2015. Some of the ceremonies have included bagpipes, a celebrant and a traditional Celtic hand-fasting.

While the Bungee Centre has become particularly well-known for its giant bridge swing (known as 'The Highland Swing'), it has had many other claims to fame. Its oldest jumper to date has been 90-year-old Bob Steel, who enjoyed a bungee experience in 2013, while jumps have been hosted

in a variety of different scenarios including participants playing the blues guitar, in a kayak, on a BMX bike, and even when playing the bagpipes! The centre and its staff have featured on Dutch TV, in adverts for Singapore Airlines, and have even appeared in a Bollywood movie. When part of *Outlander*'s season 4 was being filmed in and around Killiecrankie in 2018, many of the cast members decided to take the chance of their own personal bungee jump while they were staying at the village.

Another popular feature of Killiecrankie has been Scottish Quads (*www.scottishquads.co.uk*), considered by many to be among Scotland's premier quad-biking experiences. From quad treks to full-day adventures, the company can accommodate everything from single-person events to group activities. Making the most of Highland Perthshire's amazing scenery, the company doesn't just offer quad-biking – other activities provided include white-water rafting, canyoning, paintball and much more besides, to please every outdoor enthusiast.

Chapter Four

The Riverside East

THE Rivers Tummel, Braan, Ericht and Tay provide the picturesque backdrop to the stunning natural scenery along this section of the Heart 200. This is the perfect area for riverside walks, such as an amble to the River Tummel from Pitlochry or a leisurely saunter to the Hermitage waterfall on the River Braan near Dunkeld. You also won't want to miss a visit to the area's other eye-catching natural attractions such as Cargill's Leap on the River Ericht at Blairgowrie or the famous Loch of the Lowes Nature Reserve near Dunkeld where visitors can see ospreys at certain times of year, as well as beavers and red squirrels. Returning to the River Tay, don't forget to take time out to visit Stanley Mills or the exquisite Scone Palace, set in its own grounds on the river's eastern banks. From food lovers to those seeking outdoor adventure, the Riverside East has something unique to offer you.

Pitlochry

One of the highlights of the Heart 200 route, there is never any shortage of things to see and do in Pitlochry – whatever your interests may be. Pitlochry is a town famous for its links to the Victorian era, when Queen Victoria and Prince Albert visited the area in 1842 on their way to purchase their Highland estate at Balmoral. Though the town grew up around its railway station, which was founded in 1863, older settlements such as Port-na-craig and Moulin predate it by many centuries. The town as we know it in modern times didn't

begin to take its familiar shape until its famous military road was constructed in the 18th century, which eventually led to the two previously-distinct communities becoming more closely intertwined. After many decades of welcoming visitors, the town remains a popular tourist resort which offers plenty of eye-catching walking destinations as well as its numerous contributions to arts and culture. It became a burgh in 1947.

Pitlochry has had no shortage of famous connections beyond its royal association. Author Robert Louis Stevenson was a guest at the town's Fishers Hotel in the summer of 1881, while radar pioneer Sir Robert Alexander Watson-Watt FRS (1892-1973) and his wife Dame Jane Trefusis Forbes (1899-1971) – the founding Director of the Women's Auxiliary Air Force, from 1939 to 1943 – regularly stayed at their summer house in the town (known as 'The Observatory'). After Forbes was bequeathed the house from her uncle, physicist George Forbes, in 1936, she temporarily offered it

as a place of short-term rest and respite for senior military officers during the Second World War, with Field Marshal Bernard Montgomery KG, GCB, DSO (1887-1976) believed to have been one of its guests. Alexander MacKenzie (1822-92), who would become the second Prime Minister of Canada, was educated at a parish school in Moulin.

A useful first port of call for visitors may well be the Pitlochry VisitScotland iCentre (*www.visitscotland.com/info/services/pitlochry-icentre-p234421*) in the town's Atholl Road, which is amply stocked with information about the region, its heritage and the many things to see and do here. Pitlochry has become especially well-known for Pitlochry Festival Theatre (*www.pitlochryfestivaltheatre.com*), situated on Port-na-craig Road, which offers a wide range of entertainment including live performances. In the summer, the theatre famously presents half a dozen plays in daily repertory which means that audiences have the opportunity to see six different plays over six consecutive

nights. Originally the brainchild of John Stewart, one of Glasgow's foremost advocates of amateur dramatic productions, the theatre opened in May 1951 and has gone from strength to strength ever since. Initially a tent-style theatre, a custom-built structure was constructed on the site and opened in May 1981 on the theatre's thirtieth anniversary. It is currently undergoing a further, ambitious expansion which is expected to be complete in time for the theatre's seventieth anniversary in 2021. Pitlochry Festival Theatre is one of the most culturally important organisations in all of Perthshire, so checking their schedule of performances ahead of time, and booking tickets for events in advance, is highly advised.

Located just behind the Festival Theatre is the celebrated Explorer's Garden (*www.explorersgarden.com*). Dubbed 'The Scottish Plant Hunter's Garden', this horticultural treasure trove is the ideal place for visitors to learn stories of the people who risked their lives in years past to find new plants and trees for cultivation and conservation. In addition to garden tours, several workshops take place here including Scottish gin tasting, tea tasting, and instructional tutorials such as 'How to Grow a Himalayan Blue Poppy'. Other events are organised throughout the year, including photographic exhibitions. Don't forget to admire the incredible view from the Moongate when you visit. To find out how to participate, availability and dates can be checked online.

Pitlochry Hydroelectric Dam Visitor Centre (*www.pitlochrydam.com*) in Armoury Road showcases the long and rich history of hydroelectric power in the North of Scotland, and explores the many ways in which it has transformed lives. The visitors centre highlights not just the historical figures who made hydroelectricity a reality in the area, such as politician Tom Johnston CH, FRSE (1881-1965) and the Tunnel Tigers construction teams, but also features numerous fascinating exhibits which bring the subject to life. The centre

also features a 310-metre long 'fish ladder', where salmon can be seen making their way back upstream to their breeding ground. This was part of the scheme's design in the 1950s, and guests can now discover more about the amazing journey of the salmon and their life-cycle at the centre.

Since opening in 2017, the Pitlochry Dam Visitor Centre has already welcomed over 300,000 guests at time of writing. The force on the dam is around 12,000 tonnes – equivalent to six space shuttles! Much of the dam is not visible from the surface – some 80% of the structure is actually underwater, as its foundations are a further 60 feet below what can be seen from the café's balcony. Incredibly, water powering the hydroelectric dam may have been used up to four times already through upstream hydro stations before it reaches Pitlochry. One little-known fact is that contrary to popular myth, the salmon don't actually leap up the fish ladder, but rather swim along a series of tunnels. However, it's entirely possible to see them jumping around in the river! The centre's operat-

ing hours change in the winter months, so please check the centre's website ahead of your visit.

Located in the heart of Pitlochry at Tower House, Station Road, the Wild Space Visitor Centre (*www.johnmuirtrust.org/our-work/wild-space-visitor-centre*) is operated by the John Muir Trust and offers unique interpretative exhibitions and audio journeys. Featuring an informational presentation and exclusive audio journeys which showcase famous Scottish destinations including Ben Nevis and the Isle of Skye, the Wild Space Visitor Centre is a great destination for all nature enthusiasts. There are also regular exhibitions in the John Muir Trust's Alan Reece Gallery, which displays a changing range of artworks created by a variety of artists during the year. Numerous events take place at the centre at different times, including organised walks, presentations and family activities.

Pitlochry is home to one of Scotland's oldest distilleries, the renowned Blair Athol Distillery (*www.malts.com/en-row/distilleries/blair-athol/*), which dates back to 1798. As well as sampling the fine single malt on the premises, visitors can take part in a multiplicity of different tours, tasting tours and guest experiences. The distillery's ancient water source is the Allt Dour, a pure water supply which encouraged the company's founders – John Stewart and Robert Robertson – to establish their business in Pitlochry in the late 18th century. Blair Athol Distillery has had a long and intriguing history which guests can learn about in more detail with a visit to the visitor centre, established in

1987. Some rare and remarkable whiskies can be experienced at the distillery's famous Mash Tun Bar. Opening hours vary throughout the year, so it is recommended to confirm availability in advance.

Whisky connoisseurs will also want to check out the Edradour Distillery (*www.edradour.com*), which is famously one of Scotland's smallest distilleries. Founded in 1825 and drawing its water source from Ben Vrackie Springs, the distillery is located on the banks of Edradour – a small burn from which it takes its name. The company has become famous for the huge diversity of its whisky range, in addition to its well-known cream liqueur containing Edradour whisky. The visitor centre on the premises, which offers tours, is open from April until October. Real ale enthusiasts may prefer a trip to the popular, compact Moulin Brewery (*www.moulinhotel.co.uk/inn/brewery.html*) – a microbrewery situated only a short walk away from Pitlochry's railway station. Opened in 1995, the company has become a firm favourite with aficionados on account of its varieties of ale, which include Ale of Atholl, Old Remedial Ale and Braveheart Ale. Brewery tours are available on weekdays, but it is best to book in advance – and essential if your group comprises of more than six people.

A leading independent specialist merchant in whisky, gin and spirits, Robertsons of Pitlochry (*www.robertsonsofpitlochry.co.uk*) is one of the premier tasting venues in Scotland. Located in the town's Atholl Road, the shop is open seven days a week and stocks over 450 top whiskies, more than 150 craft gins, and in excess of 50 of the finest rums. Tasting experiences can be arranged for private groups both small and large, though it is recommended to contact the company in advance for details of available dates and pricing.

A stockist of truly unique handcrafted Scottish jewellery, ornamental items and gifts, Heather Gems (*www.heathergems.com*) is located on Atholl Road just behind the town's tourist information centre. Their factory shop and visitor centre allows guests to discover more about the techniques which lie behind the creation of these exclusive artworks, which are crafted from natural Scottish heather. The company is the only manufacturer of these wonderful creations in the world, and this has been the case since the business was founded in the 1950s. Depending on the time of your visit, skilled craftspeople can be seen in action creating the jewellery on the premises.

Scottish history devotees certainly won't want to overlook a visit to the historic Atholl Palace Museum (*www.athollpalace.com/museum-atholl-palace*). Situated on Atholl Road in what was once the old servant's quarters of Atholl Palace – now the Atholl Palace Hotel – this is a terrific place to learn more about Victorian history. The highly entertaining exhibitions follow the history of the hotel from its early days as a hydropathic spa in the 1870s, including its conversion into a school for evacuees during the Second World War and its later reopening to the public. The museum is open daily throughout the week. The 19th century manor house itself has been converted into a top hotel with a luxury spa and expansive, award-winning gardens.

Historical and archaeological interest is also firmly at the heart of the Pitlochry and Moulin Heritage Centre (*www.pitlochryandmoulinheritagecentre.co.uk*), based in Moulin Kirk on Moulin Square. With afternoon opening hours from May to October, this fascinating visitor experience invites its guests to take a trip back in time to ancient life in the area, including Moulin's medieval Black Castle, the flax industry and the old trades of Pitlochry. Historical photographs and postcards are on display, along with newspaper articles and even school class photos from bygone decades. For anyone with an interest in Highland Perthshire, and

Pitlochry and its surrounding area particularly, the centre is a veritable treasure trove.

On the shores of beautiful Loch Faskally, Pitlochry Boating Station and Adventure Hire (*www.fishfaskally.com*) is a family-run business which operates between March and October, Mondays to Sundays, that offers a wide range of outdoor activities. This includes pedalo hire, boats with outboards, and kayaks. Fishing permits are available, as is spinning rod hire. For those who prefer to stay on the ground rather than the waves, the company offers mountain bike rental. Outdoor adventures are also very much on the agenda at Perthshire Treks (*www.perthshiretreks.scot*), where extraordinary walking experiences are available around Perthshire and beyond. Established by outdoor experts Brenda Clough and Richard Davison, the company's mission is to provide unique walking adventures which are enjoyable, safe and informative. Their many guided walks include destinations offering natural beauty such as waterfalls, hills, scenic views and the many hidden secrets of the

region. Visitors should call ahead of time to arrange their bespoke walking adventure and find out about fees for individual participation and group costs.

For those seeking a more serene experience during their visit to the area, Pitlochry features a peaceful and beautifully-maintained Memorial Garden (*www.inspirock.com/united-kingdom/pitlochry/pitlochry-institute-park-war-memorial-and-memorial-garden-a4462539839*) which is centrally located in Atholl Road. The gardens are adjacent to the town's War Memorial, established in honour of those citizens of the town who died defending their country in wartime. There are many other walks and places of beauty to suit walkers and hikers at all levels of experience. Ben Vrackie, the Queen's View, Faskally Wood and the impressive waterfall at Black Spout Wood are all popular walking destinations in the vicinity of Pitlochry. Other sightseeing locations in the area include Glen Tilt, Linn of Tummel, the Allean Forest, and Neolithic sites at Croft Moraig and the Pictish Dunfallandy Stone. The suspension footbridge over the River Tummel, built in 1913, offers stunning views

of the surrounding area. Experienced walkers will also want to note that the town is situated at the far eastern end of the Rob Roy Way.

Featuring artisan produce and crafts, Pitlochry Market (*www.pitlochrymarket.co.uk*) operates from Pitlochry Business Centre in Armoury Road on the third Saturday of the month between April and October, from 10am until 3pm. For precise dates when the market takes place throughout the year, please check their website. Arts and culture events taking place in Pitlochry include the Enchanted Forest (*www.enchantedforest.org.uk*) sound and light show at Faskally Wood every autumn; the town's annual literary festival, the Winter Words Festival (*www.pitlochry.org/events/winter-words-festival.html*), which takes place in

late winter; and Pitlochry Highland Nights (*www.torrdarach.co.uk/pitlochry-highland-night/*) – music and dance events organised over the summer months by the Vale of Atholl Pipe Band.

Other events taking place in Pitlochry throughout the year include closed-roads sportive Etape Caledonia (*www.etapecaledonia.co.uk*) in the spring; music festival *March into Pitlochry* (*www.marchintopitlochry.co.uk*); Pitlochry Highland Games (*www.pitlochryhighlandgames.co.uk*) every September; the Gents and Ladies Highland Open competitions at Pitlochry Golf Course (*www.pitlochrygolf.co.uk*); and even a lively annual Christmas Festival (*www.pitlochry.org/events/christmas-festival.html*). Please consult with tourist information for details about times and dates for these events, and other seasonal activities taking place in and around the town.

Ballinluig and Grandtully

The villages of Ballinluig and Grandtully offer something for the historically-minded and the outdoor activities enthusiast alike. Scenic and captivating Ballinluig is situated on the banks of the River Tummel, and was originally developed during the construction of the Highland Railway where it was an important transport link to Aberfeldy. Today, it features the well-regarded Tynreich Nursery garden centre (*www.tynreichnursery.co.uk*), with its wide variety of plants, shrubs and trees for sale, and the popular Ballinluig Services and Motor Grill (*www.ballinluigservices.co.uk*).

Situated on General Wade's Military Road, the long-established Nae Limits Activity Centre (*www.naelimits.co.uk*) is an outdoor activity hub which offers canyoning, white water rafting, tubing and quad biking, alongside many other adventures both on land and on the waves. Numerous packages are available, with special emphasis on team activities and even stag and hen weekends. For younger visitors, the Wee Limits Adventures Academy presents a range of outdoor pursuits for younger guests aged 5 to 12. The centre is very popular, so visitors are advised to check ahead for availability before their visit.

Grandtully (commonly pronounced 'Grantly') is a picturesque village near the River Tay, with two bridges spanning the river – the Old Bridge and the more recent Pitnacree Bridge. Grandtully was the birthplace of Major George Stewart (1831-68), the famous Victoria Cross winner who fought in the Crimean War with the 93rd Sutherland Highlanders.

The historical gem of St Mary's Chapel (*www.historicenvironmentscotland.scot/visit-a-place/places/st-marys-church-grandtully*), built by Alexander Stewart around the year 1533, is situated in Nether Pitcairn. A remarkably-preserved 16th century church, its modest exterior and remote location outside the village give little hint of the amazing sight which lies within its unassumingly austere

confines: bright tempera paintings that adorn its wooden tunnel vault ceiling, dating all the way back to the 17th century. The array of vibrant Renaissance-style renderings, which depict Biblical characters and scenes along with coats of arms and other details, were painstakingly restored in the 1950s and are essential viewing for any admirer of Scottish history who happens to be visiting the area.

The foundations of the original Grandtully Castle, which was constructed in or around 1414, can be found in grounds to the east of the town, around one mile east of the current castle. The distinctive Z-plan Grandtully Castle (*www.thecastlesofscotland.co.uk/the-best-castles/other-articles/grandtully-castle*) which stands today was originally built as a three-storey tower house in 1560, but was extended in 1626. The Earl of Mar stayed at the house during the Jacobite Rebellion of 1715, and the castle was later visited by Bonnie Prince Charlie during the 1745 Rising. Considered to be the inspiration for the house of 'Tully-Veolan' in Sir Walter Scott's famous *Waverley* cycle of historical novels (1814-32), the building was renovated and modernised in the 1920s and has since been converted into a series of privately-owned apartments, so it is not accessible to the public for viewing.

Those seeking the more adventurous life will want to check out the Freespirits Outdoor Company (*www.freespirits-online.co.uk*) in Grandtully, where white water rafting on the River Tay is the order of the day. However, Freespirits offers a wide variety of activities beyond watersports such as kayaking and canyoning; on-land pursuits including abseiling, cliff jumping and bungee jumping are also catered for. Many activities are available, under the supervision of the company's experienced

staff, so be sure to consult their website for the price and availability of their packages.

The beautiful and fast-moving Grandtully Rapids (*www.ukriversguidebook.co.uk/rivers/scotland/centra-highlands/river-tay-sca-access-point-to-grandtully*) have become a famous site for rafting and canoeing, and is divided into four discrete sections: the top falls, the middle rapids, the 'boat breaker', and the fourth falls. The Scottish Canoe Association runs a campsite near the rapids, including the amenities of the Jack Cuthill Building (named for the first commodore of the Forth Canoe Club), which is a popular destination for watersports enthusiasts.

Anyone with a sweet tooth may well find themselves more inclined to visit the busy premises of Iain Burnett: The Highland Chocolatier (*www.highlandchocolatier.com*), a leading tourist attraction which includes an opulent chocolate lounge, well-stocked gift shop and an instructional chocolate exhibition (including an audio guide).

Iain Burnett is an internationally award-winning master chocolatier, and visitors have the chance to browse his shop and purchase items from his outstanding range of handmade artisan confections which include truffles, pralines, dipped fruits and caramels, to say nothing of his famous chocolate creations. The company's multimedia presentation will reveal just how they have turned chocolate-making into a true art-form. Larger groups are asked to contact the company in advance to arrange bookings for their visitor experience.

Dunkeld and Birnam

The twin villages of Dunkeld and Birnam, straddling the River Tay, are linked by a seven-arched bridge which was built by Thomas Telford in 1809. Dunkeld, on the northern bank, has the distinction of being the smallest cathedral city in Scotland, with a population of just over a thousand people. The area is famed for its beautiful riverside walks, not least to the Birnam Oak which can be found on the scenic Birnam Riverside Path (*www.walkhighlands.co.uk/perthshire/birnam.shtml*), which runs along the banks of the River Tay. The Birnam Oak and its similarly impressive neighbour, the Birnam Sycamore, are thought to be the sole surviving trees of the great forest that once straddled the banks and hillsides of the River Tay. This area is celebrated in William Shakespeare's 1606 play *Macbeth* as the famous Birnam Wood, which has immortalised the village in popular culture.

Dunkeld has a long history, with its establishment believed to date back to the time of Constantín mac Fergusa, King of the Picts (who reigned from 789 to 820AD) – though a Pictish monastery was already thought to exist on the site at that time. The later medieval cathedral came to occupy great religious prominence in eastern Scotland. The village was badly damaged during the Battle of Dunkeld in August 1689, when the Jacobites fought the 26th (Cameronian) Regiment of Foot. Though the battle led to a Jacobite retreat, the Cameronian Regiment's commanding officer, Lt. Colonel William Cleland (1661-89), was mortally wounded during the conflict. Also a noted poet, Cleland was laid to rest in Dunkeld Cathedral. The external fabric of the cathedral building still shows damage from the battle even now, centuries later.

Today, Dunkeld is considered one of the best-preserved 18th century villages in all of Scotland, considered significant among architectural historians due to the excellent conservation of the 18th century façades of many of its buildings. Visitors won't be able to miss the brightly coloured 'little houses' of Dunkeld, which were built in the early 1700s. Restored to provide homes for local people, they are now in the care of the National Trust for Scotland (NTS). Another famous NTS

property is the Ell Shop, featuring the original iron 'ell' measure – just over a metre long – which was used for measuring cloth in days gone by. Further historical information about this fascinating area can be found at the Dunkeld Community Archive (*www.dunkeldandbirnam.org.uk/listing/community-archives*) at The Cross, Dunkeld.

Dunkeld and Birnam are noted for the many places of interest within walking distance of the villages. The Hermitage (*www.nts.org.uk/visit/places/the-hermitage*), which is well signposted on the A9, is a National Trust for Scotland-protected site in Craigvinean Forest along the banks of the River Braan. Considered one of the finest walks in Perthshire, the trail takes visitors through an impressive stand of Douglas Firs – among the tallest trees in the United Kingdom – and eventually brings them to the perfect viewing point to observe a very impressive waterfall: the legendary Black Linn Falls. Originally designed as a pleasure ground for the Dukes of Atholl (who maintained a winter retreat at Dunkeld House) during the 18th century, today anyone can enjoy the wonderful sights and sounds of this area. These include Ossian's Hall (*www.undiscoveredscotland.co.uk/dunkeld/hermitage/index.html*) – a folly constructed in 1757 and rebuilt in 1951, which contains elaborate mirrored panelling and a balcony which boasts incredible views over the Falls. The Hermitage has been host to many prominent guests over the years, including artist John Turner, composer Felix Mendelssohn and poet William Wordsworth.

Also well worth seeing is Dunkeld House Tree Trail (*www.dunkeldandbirnam.org.uk/listing/dunkeld-house-tree-trail*), a National Tree Collection of Scotland (NTCS) project which is supported by Woodland Heritage. The trail celebrates the tree heritage of the Dunkeld House Estate, and relates stories about the eighteen significant trees that grow here. The grounds of Dunkeld House Hotel were used as a location in season 4 of *Out-*

lander, doubling for the wilderness of North Carolina.

Other popular destinations for walks in the area include the amazing sights of nearby Tay Forest Park (*www.visitscotland.com/ info/see-do/tay-forest-park-p1407421*), a truly unforgettable walking experience which combines local and national mythology with beautiful woodland trails. Lovers of literature, on the other hand, may prefer a visit to the highly distinctive Corbenic Poetry Path (*www.corbenicpoetrypath.com*) – a diverse area of environmental terrain including moorland, riverbanks and woodland, where poetry meets the natural landscape to striking effect.

Dunkeld is also widely recognised for its Loch of the Lowes Visitor Centre and Wildlife Reserve (*www.scottishwildlifetrust.org.uk/reserve/loch-of-the-lowes*), where many different types of wild animals can be spotted throughout the year. Operated by the Scottish Wildlife Trust, the reserve covers an area of 98 hectares, with its star attraction being its beautiful ospreys which nest close to the centre's observation hide. Other animals to be seen on the centre's grounds include wildfowl, red squirrels and beavers. There are educational activities and visual interpretations to suit visitors of all ages, though it is recommended to check the website if you intend to see particular animals during your trip, as the best time to visit may vary depending on the season.

The Birnam Arts and Conference Centre (*www.birnamarts.com*) is a vibrant focal point for arts and culture in the area, and includes one of the village's best-known attractions: the Beatrix Potter Exhibition and Garden. This presentation showcases the celebrated illustrator and author of children's fiction, and includes plenty of exciting interactive features to keep younger visitors intrigued. The Birnam and Dunkeld area greatly inspired Beatrix Potter (1866-1943), who spent her childhood holidays in the region, and her time in the villages is thought to have informed her delightful stories as well as her lifelong interests in conservationism and the natural sciences. As well as being a hub for the arts in the area, the centre also offers a café area, a gift shop, conference facilities, and has become a popular wedding venue. Situated on Station Road, Birnham, it is only a very short walk from the village's railway station.

For thrill-seekers, the Land Rover Experience (*www.scotland.landroverexperience.co.uk*) is everything you need for a truly memorable time behind the wheel in rural Perthshire. Based at But-

terstone Loch near Dunkeld, the centre is the gateway to more than 150 miles of forest and moorland track – the perfect way to discover the stunning conservation areas of the region with an off-road experience no visitor will want to pass by. A wide range of activities are on offer, from one-hour introductory sessions to full day treks. Professional training and corporate events are also available.

Butterstone Loch is a Site of Special Scientific Interest, and is home to a diverse range of wildlife which includes red squirrels, deer and birds of prey. The vehicles used by the centre are brand new – generally less than six months old – and are bright white... at least at the start of a trek (though guests are not expected to wash the cars afterwards!). The area surrounding the welcome centre is widely considered one of the most beautiful in Scotland, and has been used as a filming location for *Outlander*. If requested, instructors from the centre can even point out the location of the series' standing stones, which enable travel through time (at least, in the fictional worlds of Diana Gab-

aldon!). All of the Land Rover instructors have been professionally trained, and have a wealth of knowledge and experience – both of driving skills and the surrounding area. For younger drivers, the company also operates the well-regarded Young Off-Roader Experience (*www.youngoffroader-scotland.co.uk*), which offers the perfect off-road activity for people aged between 11 and 17. Among the pursuits on offer are driving through deep water, negotiating obstacles and tackling slopes.

Based nearby at the Steading, Dunkeld Park, Highland Offroad Quad Treks (*www.highland-offroad.co.uk*) offers training and instruction in quad biking as well as corporate and group activities to suit all tastes. A centre of excellence for 4x4 and ATV professional driver training, Highland Offroad offers adventures regardless of your level of experience – from the total novice through to the enthusiast. Introductory sessions are on offer, along with an assault course and, later, the wide open tracks and narrow woodland trails of the neighbouring forest.

The quad trek forest is the habitat of many beautiful wild animals, and safety helmets and waterproof gear is provided in order to ensure that your experience won't be affected by the changeable Scottish weather. Quad biking at the centre is an excellent family activity, and youngsters aged 12 and over are welcome to take part. The instructors are highly skilled at building confidence even in the most inexperienced participant, to ensure that everyone has a great day out. Please check the website for details of the availability of the company's services, and to see the full range of experiences on offer.

Any devotee of watersports will surely be keen to experience the excitement of Paddle Surf Scotland (*www.paddlesurfscotland.com*) at Gladstone Place, Birnam. The company offers hire and instruction in a very distinctive pastime: stand-up paddle-boarding. Whether visitors are looking for lessons, or simply want to rent equipment, this is the ideal way to experience aquatic action in stun-

ning surroundings. Other outdoor activities in the area include Progression Bikes (*www.progressionbikesscotland.com*), based at The Smiddy, St Ninians Wynd, Dunkeld. Bespoke coaching, cycling classes and even holiday camps are available, as well as an uplift service and a shop which offers spares and repairs. Dunkeld Country Clays (*www.countryclays.co.uk*) is based at Dunkeld House Hotel and is the largest sporting clay pigeon range in Scotland – as well as being home to the highest shooting tower in the UK. With a wide range of packages and suitable for all abilities, with instruction available from trained professional staff, there are many activities available for visitors.

At Fungarth near Dunkeld, the Dunkeld and Birnam Golf Club (*www.dunkeldandbirnamgolfclub.co.uk*) is among Highland Perthshire's most scenic courses. Originally established in 1892 with a course designed by golfer Thomas Mitchell 'Old Tom' Morris (1821-1908), the current course was officially opened by the Duchess of Atholl in 1922. Since then, there have been many additions and new facilities to further enhance the club. Please visit their website for details of club rules.

Taking place at the Games Park, Little Dunkeld, the famous Birnam Highland Games (*www.birnamhighlandgames.com*) have been held annually since 1864, and features competitors taking part in a wide range of events including Scottish Highland dancing, solo piping, track and field competitions, stone-putting and caber-tossing. The Games have become especially well-known for their special events, the Kiltie Dash (a fun race open to kilt-wearing entrants) and the World Haggis-Eating Championships: a hotly-contested competition where the fastest to eat a particular amount of haggis (determined by the organisers) can win the Grand Prize!

Last but by no means least, any Scottish history buff is certain to desire a visit to the jewel in the village's crown: the majestic Dunkeld Cathedral (*www.dunkeldcathedral.org.uk*). Part medieval ruin and part modern, working Parish Church, the cathedral has stood on the north bank of the River Tay since 1260, though the building as we know it today was not completed until 1501. It stands upon the site of the old Culdees Monastery of Dunkeld, which dates back many centuries, and the site has links with Saint Columba (521-97) whose bones are believed to have been stored at Dunkeld until the time of the Reformation.

Approximately half of Dunkeld Cathedral is now in ruins, but is nonetheless the location of nu-

merous burial sites. The derelict nave and its distinctive arches can still be seen from the cathedral grounds, though this part of the grounds is closed for reasons of safety. As well as being the resting place of several Bishops of Dunkeld, other historical figures buried at the cathedral include John Stewart, the 1st Earl of Atholl (c.1440-1512) and Charles Edward Stuart, Count Roehenstart (1784-1854). One of the building's foremost attractions is the tomb of the notorious 'Wolf of Badenoch' – Alexander Stewart, Earl of Buchan (1343-1405) – which can still be seen in the cathedral's sanctuary today.

Though it has centuries of history, Dunkeld Cathedral remains a busy and well-used church even in the present day. It is the Church of Scotland parish church for Dunkeld and Birnam, and is a Crown Property maintained by Historic Environment Scotland. Sunday services take place at the cathedral every week, though in the winter months the congregation instead meets at the nearby Little Dunkeld Church. Because baptisms, weddings and

funerals all take place at the cathedral throughout the year, there are some periods where the church interior is not accessible to sightseers. Its Chapter House Museum, which is situated adjacent to the main church sanctuary, contains a collection of fascinating relics from the cathedral's monastic and mediaeval history, as well as a variety of local history exhibits. Guided tours and educational visits are available during the summer; please consult the cathedral's website for further details.

Blairgowrie

An historic market town, Blairgowrie is affectionately referred to as 'Blair' by its locals. The twin burghs of Blairgowrie and Rattray were united by an Act of Parliament in 1928. Situated on the banks of the River Ericht, the town has a very long history as a settlement with numerous excavated artefacts dating back to Neolithic times and the Bronze Age. Pinnata Castra, a Roman legionary fortress (*www.castlesfortsbattles.co.uk/perth_fife/ inchtuthil_roman_fort.html*) which dates from around 80-90AD, is located at Inchtuthil near the town and is well known as a site of great archaeological significance. The extensive collection of Pictish remains originating from this area can be seen on display at the Meigle Sculptured Stone Museum (*www.historic-environment.scot/visit-a-place/ places/meigle-sculptured-stone-museum/*), located in Dundee Road in the village of Meigle which is around five miles to the east of the town. There are 26 carved stones on display, with the oldest dating back to the 8th century and containing detailed symbolic decoration.

Blairgowrie has a proud industrial history due to its past as a flax-growing hub, its population growing vastly in the 19th century due to the prominence of its textile industry. There were no less than twelve spinning mills in operation along the River Ericht during the town's textile manufacturing heyday in the 1870s, though none remain active in the present day. Blairgowrie also had a thriving livestock market until the 1960s, and from the 20th century onwards became especially well regarded for its contribution to fruit cultivation and jam-making. In modern times, the town remains at the centre of Perthshire's soft fruit-growing industry, with its raspberries and strawberries being particularly sought after. Among the numerous noteworthy people born in Blairgowrie and Rattray are botanist Professor Robert Alexander Robertson FRSE, FLS (1873-1935), noted physician Lt. Col. Alexander Dron Stewart FRSE (1883-1969) and

folk singer and poet Hamish Henderson (1919-2002).

Situated at the heart of the town is a perennially popular outdoor venue, the Wellmeadow (*www.discoverblairgowrie.co.uk/app-not-to-miss/group-coaching*), where events and markets are regularly held. Originally a cattle watering hole, it is thought to be named after a well which was established by St Ninian during his time in the area during the 5th century. Even when it is not in use for public activities, it remains a peaceful green space amongst the hustle and bustle of everyday life. The town centre itself has a great selection of independent retailers, and new visitors to the area will want to check in at the Blairgowrie Tourist Office (*www.blairgowrie.cylex-uk.co.uk/company/tourist-information-centre-17098349.html*), located at the Wellmeadow, for the latest information to help them enjoy their stay as well as details of seasonal events and other activities taking place around town.

Blairgowrie is also the main starting point for the Cateran Trail (*www.walkhighlands.co.uk/perthshire/cateran-trail.shtml*) which walkers can follow, based around the historic drove roads used by cattle merchants. Now widely considered to be one of Scotland's greatest walking experiences, the circular Cateran Trail is divided into five sections – measuring 64 miles (103 km) in total – and can be covered in five days or less. The town also marks the start of the breathtaking Snow Roads (*www.snowroads.com*) – a 90 mile (145 km) scenic driving route through the natural beauty of Cairngorm National Park to historic Grantown-on-Spey, via towns such as Glenshee, Braemar, Ballater and Tomintoul.

Destinations for popular walks around Blairgowrie (*www.pkct.org/blairgowrie-walks*) include Kitty Swanson's Bridge, a picturesque eight mile circular route; the Darroch (or Bluebell) Woods; the Ardblair Trail, and the Knockie Path which leads to a vantage point offering an impressive vista over the town. Another remarkable feature is the Meikleour Beech Hedge (*www.visitscotland.com/info/towns-villages/meikleour-beech-hedge-p2494-01*), located four miles south of Blairgowrie and officially recognised as the highest hedge in the world. At 100 feet (30m) high and a third of a mile (530m) in length, it is a truly striking sight to behold. The hedge was established in 1745 by Jean Mercer and Robert Murray Nairne on the Meikleour Estate, belonging to the Marquess of Lansdowne. The men responsible for the actual planting of the hedge were killed in battle at Culloden, and in their memory the growth of the hedge was allowed to continue unchecked as it was thought to be reaching to the heavens.

Founded in 1889, Blairgowrie Golf Club (*www.theblairgowriegolfclub.co.uk*) is a very well-known destination for golfing visitors, especially since hosting the Junior Ryder Cup in 2014. The club is highly regarded and prides itself on being welcoming to guests, whether they are in town for a round of golf or a spot of lunch. It contains two 18-hole courses (named 'Lansdowne' and 'Rosemount') as well as a 9-hole course. Online booking facilities for visitors are available on the club's website. As well as an award-winning clubhouse, there is also a comprehensively-equipped pro shop on the premises to meet the needs of all visiting golfers.

The site of Blairgowrie's Mercat Cross – the place where towns and burghs were granted the right to hold a regular fair or market – can still be seen near the centre of town, just outside the Old

Cross Inn (an establishment founded in the mid-1860s). Blairgowrie's impressive and distinctive War Memorial (*www.iwm.org.uk/memorials/item/memorial/8546*), which can be seen at the Wellmeadow, was designed in stone and bronze by leading monumental sculptor Alexander Carrick RSA (1882-1966) and unveiled by Mrs W. MacPherson in June 1921 in memory of citizens of the town who died in combat during the First World War. It was later rededicated in 1948 after the conclusion of World War II, and then again in 1959 in honour of those who died in the Korean War.

The Blairgowrie and Rattray Highland Games (*www.blairgowriehighlandgames.co.uk*) are held in September every year, and take place in Bogles Field on Essendy Road. The Games are a major event for the town, and it is well worth coinciding your trip with them. As well as traditional events, there are also a number of attractions which vary every year (check the website for further information) in addition to trade stands.

The town is host to many annual events, running right throughout the year. These include a dynamic community market (*www.discoverblairgowrie.co.uk/community-groups/community-market*) in the summer months, organised by the Strathmore and The Glens Rural Partnership; the popular Blairgowrie and Rattray Arts Week (*www.itsbraw.scot*) in August, which showcases the best of crafts, arts, music and drama; and the Bookmark Literary Festival (*www.bookmarkblair.com*) in October. Among the many other events taking place in Blairgowrie are the Cateran Yomp (*www.scottishrunningguide.com/race/the-alliance-trust-cateran-yomp*) in June, an endurance hiking event; the Blairgowrie and East Perthshire Walking Festival (*www.walkingfestival.org*) in September; and the celebrated 'switch on' of the town's Christmas lights (*www.discoverblairgowrie.co.uk/community-groups/blairgowrie-and-rattray-illuminations*) each November. There are many more annual occasions and activities; you can find out more from the Tourist Information Centre and on the Internet.

Blairgowrie is also known as the 'Gateway to Glenshee', for those who enjoy adventurous sporting pursuits; year-round activities include skiing, mountain biking and hang-gliding. Blairgowrie Tennis Club (*www.blairgowrietennisclub.co.uk*) at the J.J. Coupar Recreation Park on Coupar Angus Road has five all-weather floodlit courts available for 'pay and play', while NSC Outdoor Adventures (*www.nscoutdooradventures.com*) at Bal-macron Farm, Meigle, offers a wide range of adventures including an introduction to wild camping, one-day expeditions, and climbing and abseiling. A wide variety of skills training sessions are also available. The sporting and leisure facilities of LiveActive Blairgowrie (*www.liveactive.co.uk/Venues/live-active-blairgowrie*) at Beeches Road include a swimming pool, sports hall and fitness gym, with a wide range of activities on site.

Only a few hundred yards away from the centre of Blairgowrie is the River Ericht, which is a popular location for fishing, canoeing and rafting. Arguably the river's main claim to fame in history is 'Cargill's Leap' (*www.walkhighlands.co.uk/perthshire/cargills-leap.shtml*). This is the point where Rev. Donald Cargill (1619-81) – minister and Covenanter – is said to have jumped across a wide chasm over dangerous rushing water to evade capture by dragoon guards in 1679. Though Cargill was born in Rattray, there has been some historical scepticism over this tradition in more recent years,

with historians noting that neither Cargill nor his pursuer, John Graham of Claverhouse (1647-89), could be confirmed beyond doubt as having been present in Blairgowrie at the time the famous leap was said to have taken place. Further compounding this uncertainty, Cargill would have been around sixty years of age at the time of the leap – casting some doubt on his athleticism. But in spite of modern day cynicism, the legend of Cargill's Leap continues to be one of Blairgowrie's best-known historical tales, with the landmark being visited regularly every year by visitors from all over the world.

Stanley

Located just north of Perth in the village of Stanley, Stanley Mills (*www.historicenvironment.scot/visit-a-place/places/stanley-mills/*) is an exactingly preserved vestige of the Industrial Revolution. Its distinctive building houses a cotton mill first founded in 1786 by Richard Arkwright on the banks of the River Tay. For two centuries, the mill produced textiles thanks to the power generated by the mighty Tay's current – first created by water wheels, and then by hydroelectric turbines. The story of Stanley Mills is one of diversification and evolution as this industrial complex gradually developed and expanded over time.

Visitors can now discover more about the history of the mills, determine many unexpected facts from the interactive presentations, and find out what it would have felt like to be on the busy factory floor as raw cotton was processed into a sought-after end product. The exhibitions concentrate not just on the gradual development of the mill complex, but also on the life experiences of the workers there. The mill is closed over the winter months, but for details of opening times and ticket prices, please consult the Historic Environment Scotland website.

Based at Stewart Tower Farm, the Stewart Tower Dairy (*www.stewart-tower.co.uk*) is a destination with a difference. Visitors are invited to visit their herd of Holstein Friesian cows, which go out to grass in May and return inside in October; each cow is milked twice daily, averaging at around 9,000 litres of milk per cow every year. And where does all this milk go? Guests can find out at the Roundhouse – a beautifully restored horse engine house, dating back to around 1840, which has now been refurbished as an ice cream parlour and coffee shop. Stewart Tower Dairy is renowned for the quality and range of its ice creams, made to a creamy, Italian gelato-style recipe. Food available at the Roundhouse includes tray-bakes and light lunches, and guests can admire the magnificent panoramic views of Perthshire... to say nothing of the farm's characterful herd of pygmy goats. Other animal attractions are available at the farm, so nature lovers won't want to miss a visit.

Located at Burnside Farm near Stanley, the always-popular Active Kids Adventure Park (*www.activekidsadventurepark.co.uk*) offers activities and events for all youngsters, from toddlers and up. With an emphasis on fun and active play, kids can enjoy a fantastic day out in the fresh air of the countryside. There is soft play, an outdoor wigwam, and even the custom-built Tractor Ted's Little Shed – the perfect place for children's parties. Different events take place at the adventure park throughout the year, and if that wasn't enough, there is also a coffee shop and toy shop on the premises for anyone seeking that special gift.

Keen walkers won't want to miss a chance at experiencing the beautiful sights and sounds of Five Mile Wood (*www.woodlandtrust.org.uk/visiting-woods/woods/five-mile-wood*), an area of woodland near Stanley which is easily accessible just off the A9. Dog-walkers in particular will enjoy this peaceful oasis, with wide paths and many different species of tree in evidence.

The very best foods and gifts that the region has to offer can be found at Taste Perthshire (*www.tasteperthshire.co.uk*), situated at Bankfoot near Stanley. This highly-rated centre contains the

Perthshire Tourist Centre for information and enquiries related to attractions in the area, but has become best-known for its food larder and deli which contain a huge array of fresh farm produce, pilled pies, fresh bread, home baking, chilled smoked meats, seafood, jams and preserves, a popular cheese counter, and much more besides. Their shopping areas present a wide variety of clothing, gifts and homeware; wines and spirits; gift hampers; and even occasional tasting sessions throughout the year. Its 120-seat restaurant is also a highly admired destination for gourmands everywhere, with breakfasts, high teas, afternoon teas and even a Sunday roast lunch served weekly.

Taste Perthshire is a must-see location for all food-lovers, and most of the local produce on sale in their shop area is actually used as ingredients in the food served in their restaurant. Most of the staff

members are local to the area, and have a comprehensive knowledge of the products on sale as well as the region in general. There are many useful and appealing extra features in evidence on the premises, including a live Internet webcam overlooking the A9, electric car charging points, and a whisky shop and drinks cellar which sells over a hundred malt and blended whiskies, local real ales, and Scottish artisan gins. Best of all, visitors can meet the Taste Perthshire Highland Cows and might – just might – be allowed to feed them during their trip!

Scone Palace

Famous throughout the world as the historic crowning place of Scotland's Kings, Scone Palace (*www.scone-palace.co.uk*) is a Category A listed historic manor house which is an unmissable destination for any tourist. Scone Palace is situated near the village of Scone and the city of Perth. Con-

structed from red sandstone and featuring a distinctive castellated roof, it remains among the very best examples of the late Georgian Gothic style to survive in Britain today.

Originally an early church and then an Augustinian monastery, the priory was granted abbey status in the 12th century and the Abbot's residence (or 'palace') was built, hence the reason why the building today retains the title of Scone Palace. Though for centuries Scotland's monarchs were crowned at Scone, the Abbey became a secular lordship following the Scottish Reformation. The current building is the result of a programme of enlargement by architect William Atkinson (1774-1839) between 1802 and 1808, with further work completed in 1842 to prepare for a Royal visit from Queen Victoria and Prince Albert.

From the 9th century (and possibly even earlier), Scone was the crowning place of Scottish Royalty, and was the location of the famous Stone of Scone – also known as the 'Stone of Destiny'.

This coronation stone is a large block of red sandstone, and has gone by many names over the years including the Tanist Stone, Jacob's Pillow Stone, and (in Gaelic) *clach-na-cinneamhain*. Weighing around 335lb (152kg), the stone was historically housed at Scone Abbey – now a ruin – and its presence ensured that Scone was at the epicentre of Scottish politics for centuries. It was last used ceremonially at the coronation of Queen Elizabeth II in 1953, and in 1996 the stone was returned to Scotland where it now resides in the Crown Room at Edinburgh Castle along with the Honours of Scotland and the Crown Jewels of Scotland. In recognition of Scone's huge significance in Scottish history, a replica of the Stone of Scone can be seen in the grounds of Scone Palace. The stone has fired many creative imaginations and has had a massive impact on popular culture, featuring in Charles Martin Smith's film *Stone of Destiny* (2008), the two-part finale 'Destiny' of the BBC's crime mystery series *Hamish Macbeth* (1997), Andrew Greig's novel *Romanno Bridge* (2008), August Derleth's Sherlock Holmes pastiche story *The Adventure of the Stone of*

Scone (1958), and many other works besides. Historians believe that 42 Kings of Scots were crowned on the stone, including Macbeth and Robert the Bruce, and Moot Hill (upon which the stone was situated) comprises of earth which was brought from across Scotland by nobles from their own lands, emptied onto the mound as a mark of respect during enthroning and crowning ceremonies. In the modern day, visitors from all over the world enjoy sitting on the replica stone to have their photos taken at this historic place.

Today, Scone Palace is a five-star tourist attraction with its lavish State Rooms open for public visits between April and September. The building is the home of the Earl and Countess of Mansfield, as it has been for over four centuries, and boasts a vast collection of rare items including clocks, ceramics and fine furnishings. Among the many noteworthy artefacts held in the Palace are an exquisite writing desk presented to the 2nd Earl of Mansfield by Marie Antoinette (1755-93) as a token of their friendship. The Earl, David Murray

(1727-1796), had served as British Ambassador to the court of France's King Louis XVI (1754-1793). Much media attention has focused upon the Palace's portrait of cousins Dido Elizabeth Belle (1761-1804) and Lady Elizabeth Murray (1760-1825), which was once attributed to the German artist Johan Joseph Zoffany RA (1733-1810) but was subsequently revealed by the BBC's *Fake or Fortune* series to have actually been painted by Scottish artist David Martin (1737-97). Belle's life has been the subject of numerous creative works, including Amma Asante's period drama *Belle* (2013) and Evadne Bygrave's stage musical *Fern Meets Dido* (2018).

Other unique objects in evidence at Scone Palace include a gateleg oak table which is believed to have belonged to King James VI and I, the oak armchair used by King Charles II for his coronation, and a bed-hanging made by Mary, Queen of Scots during her time of incarceration in Loch Leven Castle which hangs in the Lennox Room. Alongside the Palace's extensive collection of fine art, including David Wilkie's 1806 painting *The Village Politicians* and a portrait of Andrew Murray, 1st Lord Balvaird (c.1597-1644), who remains the only Church of Scotland minister upon whom a peerage was conferred, there is a significant collection of fine porcelain on display within glass cabinets in the library. The Palace also contains within its vast collections Chippendale furniture, Dresden porcelains, and a matchless collection of Vernee Martin vases.

Scone Palace has become an especially popular destination for luxury holidays, with its Balvaird Wing offering five-star self-catering accommodation for up to six guests in three en-suite rooms, with a dining kitchen and sitting room. For details of prices and availability, please consult the Scone Palace website.

Scone Palace is almost as famous for its grounds as it is for its extravagant mansion, and they are available for public viewing throughout the year. The gardens include the famous David Douglas Pinetum, containing a magnificent collection of conifers which were planted between 1848 and 1870. One of the most famous trees at Scone is a giant Douglas Fir, raised from the first seed sent home from North America by botanist David Douglas (1799-1834) who was born in Scone and after whom the tree is named. The Palace's kitchen garden was reinstated in 2014, and produces vegetables, salads and fruits which are used in the Palace kitchens to supply the coffee shop. The garden team is made up of eight full-time gardeners and

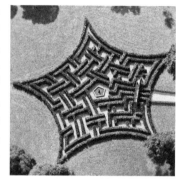

sixteen volunteer gardeners, led by Head Gardener Brian Cunningham, who is also the presenter of the BBC's *The Beechgrove Garden* (1978-).

Beautiful peacocks and peahens, sixteen in all, can be seen roaming the Palace grounds. Arguably the most famous is Alexander, a very distinctive white peacock. The birds are said to be very welcoming to visitors, and peacock food can be purchased from the Palace's food shop. The grounds are also renowned for the outstanding Murray Star Maze, created by international contemporary maze designer Adrian Fisher in 1991 and formally opened to the public by Magnus Magnusson KBE in May 1998. The maze comprises of 2,000 beech trees – half of them green and half of them copper – and at its centre is a bronze statue of the Greek nymph Arethusa set upon a fountain, designed by David William-Ellis.

It would also be remiss not to answer the important question of whether it is possible for a visitor to eat a scone at Scone. The answer is that yes, you most certainly can, and each year around 70,000 home-baked scones are sold on the premises!

In addition to its many year-round attractions, the Palace is host to a wide range of outdoor events which take place on its expansive grounds throughout the seasons. These include the Rewind Festival (*www.rewind-festival.com*); the prestigious Scottish Game Fair (*www.scottishfair.com*), and the Farming Yesteryear Vintage Rally (*www.scone-palace.co.uk/whats-on/farming-yesteryear-vintage-rally*). Many other special events take place during the year, so be sure to check the website before your visit.

The nearby village of Scone has an interesting history itself; the medieval settlement of Scone (which developed around the monastery and the royal residence) was vacated in the 19th century when the new Palace was constructed. The inhabitants were moved to a new village, originally named 'New Scone' (to distinguish it from the historical 'Old Scone', around one and a quarter miles (2km) to the east of the previous settlement's location). Now simply called Scone, the village has become a hub of flight events and aviation training in the modern day, with a number of piloting instruction and aerial tourism companies operating in the area.

Chapter Five

The City of Perth

THE cultural epicentre of Perthshire, the city of Perth offers an extraordinary mix of the ancient and the modern; one of Scotland's most ancient settlements, you won't want to miss a visit to this vibrant, contemporary city, full of welcome surprises for the Heart 200 traveller.

People have been living in Perth since prehistory, with evidence of hunter-gatherers from the Mesolithic period having settled in the area around 6000BC. Its proximity to Scone, the royal nucleus of ancient Scotland from at least the 8th century, ensured that Perth has been a place of great significance in Scotland for well over a millennium. Granted Royal Burgh status by King William I (c.1142-1214), 'The Lion', in the 12th century, Perth soon developed into one of the wealthiest burghs in Scotland and was renowned as a centre for trade with many countries including France, Belgium and the Netherlands. Its industrial reputation continued to develop after Perth Academy was established in 1760, and the arrival of the railway in the city in 1848 ensured that Perth would also be an important transport hub for Scotland.

Perth continues to build upon its long and illustrious history in many different ways. Today it is widely recognised for its thriving retail sector and its banking and insurance industries, as well as its major contributions to the arts and culture. Perth's diverse economy is reflected in the highly varied range of attractions in and around the city; from performance art to sites of historical interest, by way of leisure activities and creative pursuits, there is something here to capture everyone's attention – whatever their interests may be.

With many popular tourist destinations, Perth remains one of Scotland's most lively and exciting cities. This vibrant hub of commerce has been called home by many famous people, including novelist John Buchan, surgeon Dr James Duncan FRSE, poet William Soutar, radio DJ Desmond Carrington, comedian Fred MacAulay and athlete Eilidh Doyle, to name only a few. Boasting immense historical importance, creative influence and a manifold impact on art, music and literature, a visit to Perth will be high on the list of anyone following the Heart 200 route.

Branklyn Garden

The beautiful and tranquil Branklyn Garden (*www.nts.org.uk/visit/places/branklyn-garden*) is located on Perth's Dundee Road, and in addition to its horticultural importance the elevated location offers a striking view of the city. Only a short walk away from the city centre, the two-acre garden area was founded in 1922 by John and Dorothy Renton after they built their property, in the late Arts and Crafts style, overlooking Perth. The gar-

den was first established with the use of rare seeds that had been gathered by celebrated plant hunters such as Frank Ludlow (1885-1972) and George Forrest (1873-1932). One of the most beautiful hillside gardens in Scotland, the serene haven that we see today is testament to Dorothy Renton's legendary gardening skills. Home to several National Collections of plants, including Himalayan poppies, Cassiope and Rhododendron taliensia, Branklyn Garden remains greatly admired by botanists and is the ideal place to unwind in exquisite surroundings while admiring nature's beauty.

Perth Museum and Art Gallery

The city of Perth has a very long association with culture and the arts, and the Perth Museum and Art Gallery (*www.culturepk.org.uk/museums-and-galleries/perth-museum-and-art-gallery*) in George Street presents a unique variety of exhibitions including artwork, natural history and archaeology, as well as temporary exhibitions on a wide range of different subjects.

The museum grew around the Marshall Monument, a memorial built in 1822 to honour Perth's influential Provost Thomas Hay Marshall (1770-1808) and designed by architect David Morison (1792-1855). Opened as a library and museum in 1824, it is one of Britain's longest-established custom-built museum buildings, and an extension was opened in 1935 by the Duke and Duchess of York to host fine artwork and natural history collections. In 1965 it was declared a Category B listed building.

Perth Museum and Art Gallery showcases the very best of Perthshire's long and fascinating history, and admission is free to the public. Among Britain's oldest museums, it holds a collection of more than half a million artefacts of local, regional, national and international relevance – perhaps most famously including an Egyptian mummy and the South Corston fragment of the Strathmore Meteorite (a large meteorite which fragmented over Perthshire and struck the areas of Keithick, Carsie, South Corston and Easter Essendy in December 1917). With its intriguing exhibits and captivating artwork, a trip to Perth Museum and Art Gallery presents the perfect opportunity to learn more about the people and the events that have shaped Perth into the city we know today.

Norie-Miller Park

Situated on Riverside, close to the city centre, Norie-Miller Park (*www.perthcity.co.uk/norie-miller-park*) is an amazing attraction where natural beau-

ty and artwork come to life. Named after famous Perth-born figure Sir Stanley Norie-Miller (1888-1973), an insurance broker and the son of the similarly-eminent insurance company managing director Sir Francis Norie-Miller (1859-1947), this beautiful park is a popular venue for walks thanks to its combination of the beautifully maintained Rodney Gardens and a unique art trail which features sculptures from artists such as David Wilson, Kenny Munro and Phil Johnson. The artwork tells the story of Perth through the accomplishments of its people, and gives a unique interpretation of the city's long history and distinctive culture.

The park has also been popularised thanks to its seasonal 'Light Nights', where the riverside walk is enhanced by beautiful artificial lighting in the evenings for the perfect romantic stroll. This feature is only operated at certain times of the year, so be sure to check in advance if you want to see them for yourself. Located on South Street, the park has become well-known for its proximity to the National Heather Collection, where – with around 950 different species in evidence – the most wide-ranging collection of heather in Scotland can be witnessed in serene surroundings.

The Black Watch Museum at Balhousie Castle

Built on Perth's Hay Street in the 17th century – though prior construction on the site dates back even further, to the 12th century – Balhousie Castle (*www.theblackwatch.co.uk*) was the seat of the Earls of Kinnoull and overlooks the city's North Inch. Comprehensively remodelled by architect

David Smart (1824-1914) in the 1860s, the building was purchased by the Regimental Trustees of the Black Watch in 2009, and from that date onwards it has functioned as the Regimental Headquarters of the Black Watch as well as their Regimental Museum and Archive.

The Black Watch is Scotland's oldest Highland Regiment, and has both observed and actively taken part in many key events in world history since its establishment in 1881 when the regiment was created from the amalgamation of the 42nd Royal Highland Regiment of Foot and the 73rd Perthshire Regiment of Foot. This included comprehensive involvement in both World Wars.

The Black Watch Museum Trust is dedicated to providing education and detailed information about the history of the Black Watch and the British Armed Forces, and the public are invited to view the story of this renowned regiment through a series of exhibitions, historical artefacts and interactive displays, incorporating many first-hand ac-

counts of army life throughout the centuries. A five-star visitor attraction, the museum was fully redeveloped in 2013 and features a gift shop and the Castle Café in addition to its learning and access programme. Opening times and ticket costs can be found on their website.

Perth Leisure Pool

One of Scotland's most popular visitor attractions, Perth Leisure Pool (*www.liveactive.co.uk/Venues/perth-leisure-pool*) on Glasgow Road is the main indoor public leisure centre for the city. First opened in July 1988, it features no less than five swimming pools – including aquatic features such as flumes, bubble beds and a separate children's lagoon – as well as numerous other facilities including a health spa, sauna, fitness gym, crèche, and an outdoor playing area for children.

While the Leisure Pool is perfect for anyone who enjoys swimming and watersports, there are many other facilities to suit different leisure-time activities such as a power plates workout studio, an outdoor boot camp and core stability classes. Social circuits and social aqua circuits are fitness classes with lower intensity that provide a great way of meeting new people while keeping fit. The conveniently-situated Café Aqua is also on site, and a perfect place for those seeking to relax after taking part in a physical workout. Additionally, Perth Leisure Pool has become a well-used venue for children's birthday parties and other events; check ahead of time if you have a special occasion in mind.

The Fair Maid's House Visitor and Education Centre

Popularised by Sir Walter Scott's novel *The Fair Maid of Perth* (1828), the famous Fair Maid's House (*www.visitscotland.com/info/see-do/the-fair-maids-house-p953211*) at North Port is thought to be the oldest surviving secular building in the city, dating back to around 1475. (Scott's tale took its inspiration from the Battle of the North Inch, a staged battle observed by King Robert III and his court during September 1396, and takes place in Perth and other Scottish locations during the turn of the 15th century.) It is from Scott's novel that Perth gained its oft-used epithet 'the Fair City'. The eponymous Fair Maid of Perth has been immortalised as a bronze statue by artist Graham Ibbeson (1951-), and is located on a park bench installation at the east end of Perth High Street.

While the 'Fair Maid' of Scott's novel, Catharine Glover, was a fictional character, the glovers (that is, glove-makers) of the city historically met in this house from the 1620s for over two centuries before relocating to a meeting room in George Street in 1858. (The Glovers' Incorporation motto, 'Grace and Peace', appears above the main doorway.) The Fair Maid's House as we know it today – which is located close to the old site of the Blackfriars monastery – was heavily renovated in the late 19th century. The building, along with the adjacent Lord John Murray House, is now home to a Royal Scottish Geographical Society visitor and education centre which focuses on the fascinating subject of earth science. Visitors can learn about

continental formation, environmental variations and cartography, amongst many other topics, with informative exhibitions and interactive presentations. Between the authentic historical setting and the thoroughly modern scientific presentations which are on offer, there really is something for everyone at the Fair Maid's House. Sightseers are recommended to check the centre's opening times ahead of their visit to make sure that access will be available during their stay in Perth, as the building is generally open on a seasonal basis.

Greyfriars Burial Ground

Not to be confused with Edinburgh's Greyfriars Kirkyard (now immortalised due to the fame of a certain Skye terrier named Greyfriars Bobby), the peaceful site of Greyfriars Burial Ground (*www.undiscoveredscotland.co.uk/perth/greyfriars/index.html*) in Perth's Tay Street contains the final resting place of many honoured people from the city's long and illustrious history.

A cemetery since 1580, the site has a long connection with religion; its location had previously been the site of a Franciscan friary established in 1496 and demolished in 1559 during the Reformation. The burial grounds were extended in the 18th and 19th centuries, and interments continued there until 1978. The calm surroundings are now also a biodiversity bank with wildflowers, butterflies and other insects making their home on the premises. Follow the footpaths (positioned in 1835) to discover the sights of the weeping lady of the Kennedy Monument and the remarkable 1782 Adam and Eve Stone. Of arguably even greater interest to history enthusiasts is a collection of early gravestones – now under a shelter to aid their preservation – which date back to the 16th and 17th centuries, including the famous Buchan Stone from 1580, the year the cemetery was founded.

The North and South Inches

Outdoors aficionados will no doubt be keen to visit Perth's two historic Inches; famous green spaces at the heart of the city. The term 'inch' derives from the Gaelic term *innis*, meaning 'meadow' or 'island'. The Inches were bestowed upon the city of Perth by King Robert III (c.1337-1406) in 1377, and remain the main parks which serve the area. The two Inches are situated around half a mile (approx. 800m) apart.

The North Inch (*www.pkc.gov.uk/article/ 15322/The-North-Inch-Perth*) is the larger of the Inches, and has an area of around 54 hectares. It is situated between Bell's Sports Centre, the River

Tay and a nearby residential zone. Often used for outdoor events such as festivals, the park includes sporting facilities and a children's play area as well as a number of memorial statues. The North Inch contains several planted areas, various memorial statues, and a cycle route is also based there. The park is also home to the North Inch Golf Club (*www.northinchgolf.co.uk*), one of the oldest golfing venues not just in Scotland or the UK, but the world. Open to visitors seven days a week, the club offers a round of golf in beautiful surroundings, with its current course designed by the legendary Old Tom Morris.

The South Inch (*www.pkc.gov.uk/article/ 15316/The-South-Inch-Perth*) is a smaller park at approximately 31 hectares. It can be found between Perth railway station (just a short walk away) and the River Tay. Like its larger counterpart, it is used to host outdoor events, and also features a skate park and sports pitches as well as a scenic pond and a play park for younger visitors. There is also a series of paths across the Inch to allow greater ac-

cessibility. The South Inch is a perennially popular location for public events such as bonfire nights, firework displays, visiting circuses and fun-fairs, and many other special occasions besides.

Kinfauns Castle

Constructed between 1822 and 1826 for politician Lord Francis Gray FRSE, FRS (1765-1842) by the architect Sir Robert Smirke RS (1780-1867) in the Castellated Gothic style, the elegant sight of Kinfauns Castle (*www.parksandgardens.org/places/kinfauns-castle*) is among the most distinctive stately homes in Perthshire.

The Castle has become particularly widely recognised for its period Victorian arboretum, which is home to a number of unusual plants – most notably, its collection of specimen conifers. While the main building operated for some time as a hotel during the late 20th century, from 2004 onwards it has been a privately-owned residence. The Castle itself is a Category A listed building, while its grounds are now featured in the Inventory of

Gardens and Designed Landscapes in Scotland. The steamer RMS *Kinfauns Castle*, launched in 1899 by the Union-Castle Line, was named in honour of the building.

Situated around two miles (approx. 3km) to the east of Perth, Kinfauns Castle contains substantial parkland and woodland areas, including an extensive garden and also a walled kitchen garden south of the Castle. While the Castle itself is no longer a hotel, a popular place for visitors to stay is in the hillside above the Castle at the Towerview Coach Houses (*www.visitscotland.com/info/accommodation/towerview-coach-houses-p220941*), a quiet yet centrally-located accommodation development which allows guests to easy access to the city centre as well as the many attractive walks around the area including 'Coronation Road' (where Scotland's ancient monarchs travelled to Scone Palace on their way to be crowned). As their name suggests, the stone-built Towerview Coach Houses were originally built to house the horses and carriages for Kinfauns Castle back in the 19th century, and are now Category B listed buildings in their own right.

Another well-regarded nearby attraction is the highly acclaimed Kinfauns Stables Riding for the Disabled Association (*www.kinfaunsstablesrda.co.uk*), a custom-built riding arena suitable for all times of the year. Established in 2015 by Geoff Brown, the arena was based in the interior of a large, renovated barn at Castle Farm and was officially opened by HRH The Princess Royal in October 2016. The company prides itself on the services it provides for its participants, and are tireless in their efforts to provide a supportive, safe and enjoyable environment for people who have behavioural issues, physical disabilities, mental health problems, learning and/or sensory disabilities, or other needs that require additional support. As well as offering pony rides and pony-focused birthday celebrations (subject to availability – please check in advance), summer and autumn holiday clubs are also organised on an annual basis. The Gesby Charity, which runs the Kinfauns Stables organisation, is entirely self-funding, and their services have already improved and transformed many lives.

Perth Concert Hall

Opened in the summer of 2005, Perth Concert Hall (*www.horsecross.co.uk*) has become one of the premier arts destinations in Scotland. A successor to Perth City Hall (the city's previous large arts venue, which is currently being redeveloped) and conveniently located in the city's Mill Street – on the site of the old Horsecross Market – Perth Concert Hall hosts a very wide range of stage performances and concerts as well as many community events. It was the winner of the Scottish Design Awards for Best Building for Public Use in 2007.

The Concert Hall has a capacity of 1,186 (seated) and 1,622 (standing), which makes it the perfect venue for large, popular events. It is managed by Horsecross Arts, who also administer the nearby Perth Theatre. At various times Perth Concert Hall has been host to performances of classical music, talks and lectures, musical theatre, ballet, opera, folk music and stand-up comedy. It has also hosted numerous events of local and regional significance, including many which have raised awareness of important social issues. Advance booking is recommended for events, due to high demand; Perth Concert Hall is very well-attended at all times of the year.

The building is also home to Threshold, a digital media arts space which has been the setting for some incredible exhibitions of contemporary art. As well as the main Gannochy Trust Auditorium, the concert hall also features a number of other meeting rooms and conference spaces including the Norie-Miller Suite (which has capacity for 120 people, though it can nominally be split into two separate meeting spaces on request). Visitors to Perth Concert Hall will no doubt also welcome a visit to the Glassrooms Café, which offers menus for different periods of the day (including pre-show meals) and is an enduringly well-liked venue.

St John's Kirk

Near the centre of the city at South St John's Place can be found one of the oldest buildings in Perth: St John's Kirk (*www.st-johns-kirk.co.uk*). This church, which is a Category A listed building, is one of the most noteworthy structures in all of Perth – both in historical and architectural terms. Though the area upon which it stands has been occupied by a church since at least the 12th century, the present familiar structure was built between 1440 and 1500, though its appearance has been altered in numerous ways over the centuries. So significant was this church to the life of Perth that the city was called 'St John's Toun' during the medieval period – a fact which is still reflected in the city's famous football club, St Johnston F.C.

Famous for its tower and spire, which remain distinctive landmarks on the Perth skyline, St John's Kirk has undergone numerous changes over the years. Its collection of medieval bells is thought to be the oldest in the UK, while it was once home to the best-preserved collection of post-Reformation church plates in Scotland. (This collection still survives today, but has now been relocated to Perth Museum and Art Gallery.) Amongst church historians, St John's is celebrated for its rare 15th century brass candelabrum featuring a statuette of the Virgin Mary, which survived the Reformation. During the 19th century, during a programme of street-widening, the building's north transept was shortened to accommodate greater movement on the streets outside the church. Its sacristy and medieval south porch were also

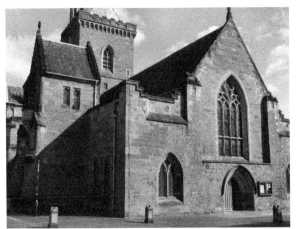

removed over the course of the centuries. The church was extensively restored during the late 19th century by the architect Sir Richard Lorimer (1864-1929).

For all its long and complex history, which is detailed in Richard Fawcett's book *A History of St John's Kirk of Perth* (1987) and several other volumes, St John's is still very much a working place of worship today with a large and diverse congregation. The church hosts regular Sunday services, worship groups and fellowship meetings, a choir, and many other community activities besides.

Elcho Castle

A remarkably preserved 16th century castle at Rhynd on the banks of the River Tay, near Perth, Elcho Castle (*www.historicenvironment.scot/visit-a-place/places/elcho-castle/*) is truly a sight to behold. Boasting three soaring towers, this fortified mansion house (which was once the home of the Wemyss Family, who remain its owners) is an unmissable destination for history buffs; though

closed over the winter months, from spring to autumn visitors can explore the castle interior and take in the truly astonishing views from its upper levels. Elcho Castle has also become well-known for its wonderful grounds and expansive orchard, which contains many traditional varieties of fruit. Interpretation boards explain the purpose and location of the walled gardens, now in ruins.

This castle provides a matchless chance to learn more about the lives of the Perthshire gentry in the late 16th century. Built around 1560 (though an earlier structure is thought to predate the existing Z-plan tower house), the interior retains a number of authentic period features including decorated plasterwork. Watch out too for the many gun-holes in evidence at ground level! There is also an original surviving 16th century 'beehive doo'cot' (dovecote), which is itself a Category A listed building. A visit to Elcho Castle is highly recommended, though it is advisable to call ahead in order to check that the site is accessible as it may be closed at short notice at times of harsh weather conditions.

River Tay Public Art Trail

Located on both sides of the River Tay within Perth city centre, the River Tay Public Art Trail (*www.pkc.gov.uk/media/20538/River-Tay-Public-Art-Trail-leaflet/pdf/River_Tay_Public_Art_Trail_leaflet*) is a remarkable collection of outdoor artwork celebrating the city and its heritage.

The artworks which make up the trail are a combination of individual pieces and design series, some of which are carved into the wall of the embankment walkway. The distinctiveness of each creation means that there is no one recommended sequence in which to view the trail; each artwork can be enjoyed in any order.

Among the most arresting of the artworks is 'Millais' Viewpoint' by Tim Shutter, located in Bellwood Park, which presents a picture frame located at a riverside viewpoint which presents a section of the Tay and its surroundings which was favoured by Victorian artist Sir John Everett Millais PRA (1829-96), one of the founders of the Pre-Raphaelite Brotherhood. Others include Shona Kinloch's eye-catching sculpture 'Eagle of Perth', commemorating the Merchant Guild of Perth's construction of the trade ship *The Eagle* to improve overseas commerce, and Lee Brewster's notable installation 'Salmon Run', which depicts the Tay flowing into the sea and salmon following the tide. Each and every one of these amazing works of art is worth your time to visit and admire.

Perth Theatre

Opening on Perth High Street in 1900, Perth Theatre (*www.horsecross.co.uk/venues/perth-theatre*) is one of Scotland's oldest custom-built theatres, and it has been renovated and expanded many times in its long and admired history. Over the years it has been the venue for countless stage dramas, musicals, revues, pantomimes and variety shows, and the theatre has featured performances by some of the great luminaries of the acting world such as Donald Sutherland, Ewan McGregor, Edward Woodward and Alec Guinness. It has been, and firmly remains, at the very centre of the city's cultural life.

Since 1966 the theatre has been home to the celebrated Perth Youth Theatre, the first theatre-based youth acting and performance group in Scotland. A Category B listed building, Perth Theatre was formally reopened in 2017 after a wide-ranging programme of redevelopment. The building now features a new entrance in the city's Mill Street to mark the restoration of the Edwardian Auditorium. The building also offers a 200-seat studio theatre in the courtyard style, spaces for creative learning activities, and dedicated community areas. The organisation prides itself on presenting the very best of local, national and international performances across all artistic forms. Perth Theatre – along with Perth Concert Hall – is managed by Horsecross Arts, a creative organisation and registered charity. Due to the very diverse range of events taking place at the theatre, tickets are highly sought after, so visitors are advised to book in advance.

Abernethy Round Tower

Located to the south-east of Perth, the village of Abernethy is home to the exceptional sight of the 12th century structure known as Abernethy Round Tower (*www.historicenvironment.scot/visit-a-place/places/abernethy-round-tower*). It remains one of only two round towers in Scotland to be built in the Irish style (the other being situated in Brechin), and historians have speculated that it may once have been a bell tower for an adjoining church which no longer exists; its location near the perimeter of the village's cemetery reinforces this theory.

Standing 22.5m (74ft) high, and with a circumference of around 5m (approx. 16.4ft), the view from the top of the tower still provides an impressive view of the surrounding area and the River Tay. Of additional historical interest is a noteworthy symbol stone, thought to be Pictish in origin, which was excavated nearby in the village and mounted onto the tower's exterior base during the

20th century. A scheduled monument, Abernethy Round Tower can only be accessed at certain times; for details of entry to the site and the availability of a key to the premises, please visit the Historic Environment Scotland website.

St Mary's Monastery and Retreat Centre

History enthusiasts will undoubtedly be eager to visit the attention-grabbing St Mary's Monastery and Retreat Centre (*www.kinnoullmonastery.co.uk*), an international, multicultural and ecumenical monastery, at Kinnoull near Perth, which is still a working place of worship and service today. At Hatton Road in Kinnoull, the centre is based away from the busy heart of the city, yet is still only a modest walk from Perth.

This listed building is an admirable example of the 19th century Neo-Gothic Revival, and its fine architecture has attracted visitors from far and wide. Completed in 1868, the monastery has had a long history as a place of training and retreat, and today it offers its visitors a period of rest and

relaxation away from the constant buzz of our busy everyday lives.

There is a range of accommodation within the centre, mostly made up of single en-suite rooms though with a number of twin rooms also available. Because the centre's grounds are located within a sizeable woodland area, the emphasis is very much on peace and repose, encouraging respite and personal replenishment.

Those seeking to explore the capacious grounds can discover more about the astonishing story of Our Lady's Well, located near the monastery. Visitors can also find out about the local services operated by the centre to serve the local community, as well as St Mary's diverse programme of courses and retreats. Please check ahead of time for the current prices and availability of rooms at the centre.

Craigie Hill Golf Club

Based at Cherrybank in Perth, the Craigie Hill Golf Club (*www.craigiehill.co.uk*) was first announced in 1911 and within two years of that date had already accrued a membership of 600 people. Under the guidance of famed course architects Joe Anderson and Willie Fernie, the course was soon acclaimed as one of the most impressively designed in Perthshire – and it continues to make an impression on players to this very day.

With a reputation for an outstandingly-maintained course, Craigie Hill Golf Club continues to offer a warm welcome to visitors, and a variety of packages for visiting parties can be purchased; for available dates, as well as the cost of green fees and equipment hire, visit the website for the most up-to-date information prior to your trip.

Huntingtower Castle

Just to the north-west of Perth, imposing Huntingtower Castle (*www.historicenvironment.scot/visit-a-place/places/huntingtower-castle*) is a grand 15th century castle which has been restored and renovated extensively over the centuries. Formerly known as the Palace of Ruthven, the building is based near the village of Huntingtower and has a long and colourful history – including times where it housed inhabitants who were accused of royal kidnap; was a destination of Mary, Queen of Scots during her honeymoon with Lord Darnley in 1565; became the home of the 1st Duke of Atholl in the 18th century; and eventually assumed its modern-day role as a family home until 2002.

Today Huntingtower Castle is in the care of Historic Environment Scotland, which invites visitors to view the Eastern Tower's wonderful 16th

century ceiling paintings (believed to originate from around 1540, they are thought to be among the earliest examples of their kind to survive in Scotland), learn about the various periods of restructuring that the castle has undergone, and discover the numerous entertaining legends associated with the building over the centuries – including the mystery of St Conval's Well. The building has a highly distinctive layout, and visitors can learn about the numerous secret hiding places – many of them exceptionally elaborate! Entry times differ depending on the season, so it is always best to check the Historic Environment Scotland website if you plan a visit.

Cairn o' Mohr Winery and Ciderhouse

One of Perth's best-kept (and best-loved) secrets, the inviting Cairn o' Mohr Winery and Ciderhouse (*www.cairnomohr.com*) is located at East Inchmichael in Errol, to the east of Perth. Cairn o' Mohr is the home of a truly outstanding range of fruit wines and local farmhouse ciders, all of which are made on the premises and which have to be tasted to be believed.

Cairn o' Mohr was founded by Ron and Judith Gillies, who opened their winery in 1987 and have never looked back since. The company's fruit wines are on sale throughout the country, and started with five popular flavours: raspberry, bramble, strawberry, oak leaf and elderberry. Many other flavours, combinations and limited editions soon followed, from the experimental to the traditional. Over the years, the Cairn o' Mohr repertoire has expanded to include Scottish bottled ciders, Pictish draft cider and many non-alcoholic beverages – including their famous Carse of Gowrie apple juice. To find out more about their legendary range of products (and their even more legendary sense of humour), a trip to Cairn o' Mohr will always entertain. Wine and cider tastings are available at their shop, there is an on-site café serving locally-sourced food, and a walk around the elderberry orchard is always a delight. Group tours are also possible by contacting the owners in advance to make arrangements.

The Fergusson Gallery

There is a reason why the building which houses Perth's Fergusson Gallery (*www.culturepk.org.uk/museums-and-galleries/the-fergusson-gallery*), based in Perth's Marshall Place, looks so distinctive – as the aquatic Latin motto above its doorway indicates, it was once a waterworks and water tower serving the city, designed by Dr Adam Anderson (1780-1846) and completed in 1832. However, this industrial architecture now contains something just as remarkable in the form of the major collection of the Leith-born artist John Duncan Fergusson (1874-1961), the famed Scottish colourist.

The Fergusson Gallery contains three galleries showcasing the acclaimed work of Fergusson and that of his wife Margaret Morris (1891-1980), considered one of the pioneers of modern dance. It was Morris who established the J.D. Fergusson Art Foundation following her spouse's death in 1961, and her unstinting efforts meant that the

gallery contains a veritable treasure trove of the artist's life which not only includes an enormous collection of his artwork (over 5,000 in all, including oil paintings, watercolours, drawings and sculptures) but also letters, books, photographs, costumes, sketchbooks and many other personal items. Due to the sheer size of the gallery's collection, not all of the exhibits and artworks are on display at the same time; the exhibitions are regularly changed for public viewing throughout the year.

Two of the building's galleries are situated in the circular waterworks structure, with the third housed in a wing adjoining the gallery on the ground floor. Gallery 1, which contains some of Fergusson's best-known artworks, can be considered an essential destination for anyone with even a passing interest in Scottish art history. The Fergusson Gallery opens seasonally, so the Perth and Kinross Council website should be consulted for details of dates when the building is accessible to the public. Admission is free of charge.

Bell's Sports Centre

One of the largest and best-equipped sporting facilities in all of Scotland, Bell's Sports Centre (*www.liveactive.co.uk/Venues/bells-sports-centre*) in Hay Street, overlooking the North Inch, offers something for everyone – from those looking to relax in their leisure-time through to the serious sporting enthusiast searching for a challenge. There is a huge range of different activities that take place at the centre, making the venue hugely popular throughout the entire year.

Bell's Sports Centre first opened in 1968, and remains instantly recognisable on account of its most prominent feature – its 17m (58ft) high dome, which is over 60m (200ft) in diameter. This made it the largest dome in Britain at the time – a fact cemented by official recognition from the Guinness Book of Records, which presented the building's architect David Cockburn with a certificate acknowledging the achievement. The centre retained this distinction until the construction of the 95m-tall (311.8ft) Millennium Dome in Greenwich, which was opened in December 1999 – originally to house the Millennium Experience exhibition. The Bell's Sports Centre building is named after famous Perth figure A.K. Bell (1868-1942), distiller and philanthropist.

The centre offers a wide variety of indoor and outdoor pursuits, including squash courts and other racquet sports, fitness classes, strength and fitness gyms, basketball, indoor cycling, football, gymnastics, pilates and power yoga, PiYo, Zumba, and many others. Many activities are also available that are particularly suitable for participants who have physical disabilities, including boccia, visual impairment football and No Limits – a multi-disciplinary sports programme for people with physical and/or sensory additional needs, including support from a trained lead coach and assistant, which comprises a number of pursuits including basketball, badminton and gym activities.

Other pastimes that are popular at the centre include the RPM filmed workout sessions, strength induction sessions, Wee Springers classes for preschool children, and the instructor-led Stride for Life walking sessions. With many opportunities to socialise as well as to take part in a huge variety of leisure-time interests, a visit to the centre's web site is highly recommended in order to see their list of activities in full. It is also worth remembering

that the centre offers much more than sports and fitness opportunities – additionally, it is home to meeting rooms, a café, and is a popular venue for children's birthday parties.

Noah's Ark Family and Entertainment Centre

Situated on Old Gallows Road, just off the A9, Noah's Ark (*www.noahs-perth.co.uk*) is a much-loved destination which makes every effort to ensure that younger visitors will have fun during their stay and retain happy memories of their time there. The family and entertainment centre is adjacent to the Noah's Ark Caravan Park, and is not located too far away from the centre of Perth.

Though the centre has become especially well-known for its soft-play areas, providing a safe and fun environment where relaxation and enjoyment is at the forefront of the experience, over the years it has expanded to include many other activities for youngsters such as a ceramics workshop, indoor karting, ten-pin bowling, slides and an exciting adventure area. The staff members pride themselves on offering a pleasurable experience for their guests, no matter what their age.

Adults may prefer a look around the well-stocked shopping area or to enjoy a snack or meal at the popular Noah's Café, which offers selections to suit all age groups. The centre is open seven days a week, but visitors are advised to check ahead of time if they intend to organise a party, and to check the website for availability and times of particular events.

Perth Race Course

Among the best-recognised jewels in Perth's crown is its famous race course (*www.perth-races.co.uk*). Based in Scone Palace Parklands, the course first opened in 1908 and remains the most northerly race track in the UK. A right-handed course which is ten furlongs (just over two kilometres) in its circumference, the race course is open 365 days a year and is famed for its many annual events.

While horse racing in Perth dates back at least until 1613, the current Perth Race Course has won many admirers due to its thoroughly modern facilities and wide range of races – boasting more than 120 events every year. From Ladies Day in May through to their Summer Carnival in August, the course has something to interest the sporting enthusiast in all of us, with visitors from all over the world arriving to admire the famous steeplechase course, hurdle course and chase course.

In addition to offering an unforgettable day at the races, Perth Race Course has also established a rock-solid reputation as one of the most impressive conference venues in Perthshire, providing meeting venues and facilities for groups of delegates ranging from 40 up to 400 – perfect for everything from team-building exercises through to full-fledged exhibitions. And if that wasn't enough, meals are served at the on-site Tay Bistro and Galileo Restaurant; the former offers delicious food right in the heart of the action next to the Parade Ring, while the latter offers stunning panoramic views of the race course and surrounding area. For details of how to book a table in advance of your trip, please visit the Perth Race Course website.

The Jardine Gallery and Workshop

The famous and much-admired Jardine Gallery (*www.julianjardine.co.uk*) at 45 New Row in Perth is owned by the acclaimed ceramic sculptor Julian Jardine, who has been delighting the public with his characterful animal sculptures since 1993. While his expressive and highly distinctive work can be viewed at his gallery, it also includes the artwork of more than forty other artists – not just from around the British Isles, but also originating from overseas.

Since 2013, the Jardine Gallery has been particularly well-known for its workshop at 38 New Row – directly across from the gallery – which offers a large (and expanding) range of instructional courses for those who are seeking first-time creative education through to experienced artists intending to fine-tune their skills. Among the many activities offered are sketching, painting, clay sculpting and watercolours. Beyond instruction for adults, the workshop offers courses suitable for children and

has become an increasingly popular venue for birthday parties. Group activities are available, and a number of events take place throughout the year – so it is important to consult the website's news page for details of forthcoming courses and special occasions. Art has unparalleled potential to awaken the creative drive in everyone, and the Jardine Gallery has built up significant expertise over the years in encouraging inventiveness, craft skills and inspiration in its guests. If you're visiting Perth, it's a destination you certainly won't want to pass by.

Kinnoull Hill

One of the most iconic sights in Perth, Kinnoull Hill (*www.visitscotland.com/info/towns-villages/kinnoull-hill-woodland-park-p249241*) towers over the city at a height of 222m (728ft). The hill has been a popular walking destination for centuries, not least on account of the stunning views it offers from its south-facing cliff summit which shows (on a clear day) the River Tay, the Tay Coast railway line and the Friarton Bridge.

Now situated in an extensive area of woodland that bears its name, Kinnoull Hill Woodland Park comprises five hills to the east of Perth: namely Corsiehill, Barn Hill, Deuchny Hill, Binn Hill and Kinnoull Hill itself. Kinnoull Hill is the tallest of the five, and has now been named a Site of Special Scientific Interest. It was opened as Scotland's first officially-recognised woodland park in 1991, and is managed in partnership between Perth and Kinross Council and the Scottish Forestry Commission.

In addition to its beautiful variety of tree species, the area is widely admired for its diverse range of wildlife – in fact, there is even a Squirrel Walk for animal lovers hoping to spot some bushy-tailed friends in their natural habitat. As well as waymarked nature trails and grassy pathways for walkers, the woodland is also a highly admired place for horse-riders and cyclists; check online with tourist information for details. Art lovers will also want to keep their eyes open for fourteen woodland sculptures created by Scottish Open Chainsaw Carving Champion Pete Bowsher, which are located around the park and reflect its amazing flora and fauna.

The hill is also the site of the historic Kinnoull Tower (*www.walkhighlands.co.uk/perthshire/kinnoull-tower.shtml*), an 18th century folly constructed by the 9th Earl of Kinnoull (1710-87) and modelled after Rhineland castles that he had seen when touring Germany. Alongside its eye-catching castellated round tower, the folly also in-cludes battlements and arches. Kinnoull Tower was gifted to the city of Perth in 1924.

Moncrieffe Island

Situated in the River Tay and dividing the tide of water into two channels as it flows through Perth, Moncrieffe Island (*www.scottish-places.info/features/featurefirst9767.html*) is one of the most instantly-recognisable landmarks in the city. Also known as Friarton Island, this leafy land mass will always have a historic claim to fame in Perth due to it having once been the location of a filter bed to source engineer and schoolmaster Dr Adam Anderson's innovative early 19th century strategy to provide the city with a clean source of drinking water by pumping it to the waterworks building in Marshall Place (now the Fergusson Gallery) for purification; a pioneering scheme which was well ahead of its time.

Today, Moncrieffe Island has become renowned as the home of the King James VI Golf

Course (*www.kingjamesvi.co.uk*), which was originally established in Perth's South Inch in 1858 before the course was eventually relocated to Moncrieffe Island in 1897, where it remains to this day. Named for arguably Scotland's most famous royal advocate of the game of golf, King James VI and I, the superbly-maintained course was designed by Old Tom Morris, and its island-based location has made it one of the most distinctive places in Scotland to play a round. The clubhouse and golf shop are also accessible on-site. Information for visitors and an online booking form are available on their website.

The remainder of the island's surface area has been occupied by an array of private allotment gardens (*www.yourcommunitypk.org/listing/allot-ment-moncrieffe-island/*) since 1896. Containing 58 full plots and 13 half plots – with each plot being divided into an area of around 210 square metres (250 square yards) – the allotments are operated by Perth Working Men's Garden Association.

The Dewar's Centre
Based at Glover Street in Perth, the Dewar's Centre (*www.liveactive.co.uk/Venues/dewars-centre*) prides itself on its reputation as 'The Home of Scottish Curling'. Celebrated for its Olympic-standard ice rink, curling takes place at the centre between September and March – and the centre was famously one of the training rinks used by the Olympic medal-winning curling team led by Eve Muirhead prior to the 2014 Winter Olympics. The centre is also used for public ice skating during this period, and ice lessons are available for private clients. Other activities taking place at the centre include indoor bowls, pilates and yoga.

The Dewar's Centre has also developed considerable prestige for its extensive meeting and conference facilities, with two large conference halls and five meeting rooms providing a wide range of options for venue hire. The centre has a range of audio-visual equipment on site for use in presentations, and with over three hundred car parking spaces on the premises it has become one of the most sought-after conference venues in the area. There is a licensed bar on the premises which is perfect for organising a celebratory event or other special occasion in style.

The A.K. Bell Library
Named in honour of Arthur Kinmond Bell (1868-1942), Perth's famous distiller and philanthropist, the A.K. Bell Library (*www.culturepk.org.uk/venues/ak-bell-library/*) is situated at Perth's York

Place and was officially opened in 1995. In his lifetime, Bell was a hugely successful managing director of Arthur Bell & Sons Ltd., the whisky distillers, and became known throughout Scotland and beyond for his unstinting philanthropic efforts – which included the establishment of the charitable Gannochy Trust in 1937. He was presented with the Freedom of Perth in 1938, which – not least given the great pride he placed in his home city – he considered to be the greatest honour of his life.

The A.K. Bell Library is currently the largest community library in Perth and Kinross, and is also the headquarters of Culture Perth and Kinross: a charitable trust responsible for the delivery of many cultural services including family and local history, creative learning, community archives, libraries and museums. The historic exterior gives some hint of the building's origins as the Perth County and City Infirmary constructed between 1834 and 1848, but the structure was greatly extended between 1992 and 1994 to accommodate its new function as a cultural and informational hub.

In addition to the extensive range of books belonging to the library, the building also houses collections from the Perth and Kinross Archive, a local and family history collection, and considerable reference resources including newspapers and magazines. There are Internet and computer facilities available on-site, and a popular library café. The building also houses the 125-seat custom-built Soutar Lecture Theatre, and two highly adaptable meeting rooms: The Mackenzie Room and the Sandeman Room. Please check the library's website for details about how to access the many facilities available on the premises.

Perth Playhouse

Designed by the famous Kingussie-born architect Alexander Cattanach Jr (1895-1977) and first opened to the public back in 1933, the distinctive Art Deco exterior of the famous Perth Playhouse (*www.perthplayhouse.co.uk*) makes it one of the most unique sights in the city's Murray Street. However, this Category B listed building contains far more than first meets the eye. Becoming an independent cinema in 2014, the Playhouse has continued to develop over the decades and now houses seven screening rooms. The largest, Screening Room 1, is home to a state-of-the-art IMAX screen which is some 60% larger than the room's original projector screen. (Perth Playhouse was only the fourth cinema in Scotland to use IMAX technology on its premises.)

Perth Playhouse presents a very wide range of different cinematic entertainment throughout the year, and checking the schedule on their website and booking ahead of time is advised before your visit to the city. Alongside the latest film releases are screenings of

documentaries, live broadcasts, themed retrospectives, dementia-friendly presentations, and special events. Perth Playhouse really does present a first-class line-up, and a visit to this perennially popular destination will no doubt be on the list of many sightseers during their stay in the city.

The Willowgate Activity Centre

Just to the south-east of Perth, at Stockgreen Lodge in Lairwell, Kinfauns, Willowgate Activity Centre (*www.willowgateactivitycentre.co.uk*) is a multi-function adventure hub which offers plenty to see and do – whether you prefer fun in the water or on dry land! Right next to the River Tay, it has become particularly well-regarded for its water-based leisure activities including aqua zorbing, paddle-boarding, kayaking and canoeing. The centre's guided river trips are also highly sought-after.

However, for those who prefer *terra firma* there is also bike hire, target and field archery, a variety of team-building exercises, and an instructional series focusing on outdoor education and bush craft – including animal tracking, fire lighting and water filtration – led by skilled experts. And once you've tired yourself out with all of the adventure activities on offer, you have the option of retiring to the cosy Willowgate Café for a wide range of delicious homemade foods.

The Willowgate Activity Centre has proven to be popular for school trips, hen and stag nights, corporate events and birthday parties, and fishing sessions on the Tay are also available – check with the staff in advance for details.

Perth Cathedral

Located in North Methven Street in the busy heart of the city, the impressive Perth Cathedral (*www.perthcathedral.co.uk*) is one of the most striking architectural sights in Perth. Also known as the Cathedral Church of St Ninian, this Category A listed building is operated by the Scottish Episcopal Church and was first consecrated in 1850 – though it was later greatly extended to the designs of architect John Loughborough Pearson (1817-97), with work continuing between 1900 and 1908 and further extensions to the cloisters being added in 1936. The cathedral building is especially well-known for its superb stained glass, including the east window's detailed evocation of a scene from the Book of Revelation designed by London-based architect William Butterfield (1814-1900) and created by stained glass artist Alexander Gibbs (c.1832-86) which was added in 1876.

Perth Cathedral remains a highly active place of worship in the present day, and offers church services throughout the week. It has a long and rich history, not least with music – there is a highly respected Cathedral Choir, a junior choir named the St Ninian's Choristers, and a majestic church organ which was rebuilt and restored in 1996. The cathedral is also highly active in community matters, including Traidcraft (an organisation fighting poverty through trade), Perth and Kinross Association of Voluntary Service (PKAVS) and a highly active Eco Group which raises awareness of sustainable living and environmental issues.

Virgin Balloon Flights

By now, you've read about some of the incredible things to do in Perth... and what better way to see this amazing and vibrant city but from the air? With a launch site right at the centre of Perth, Virgin Balloon Flights (*www.virginballoonflights.co.uk/location/perth-city-centre*) offers the chance to see the city from a truly outstanding vantage point – all from the safety of a hot air balloon

– with a wide variety of different packages available. Based in the North Inch, visitors can see the famous landmarks of the city – from Balhousie Castle to the Fair Maid's House – as well as many landmarks beyond Perth, such as Scone Palace and Elcho Castle.

Balloon flying season takes place between March and October, and customers purchase their flight vouchers in advance of their trip. Flights are scheduled four to six weeks in advance, and – while changeable weather conditions mean that a flight cannot always be guaranteed – in the event that a flight is cancelled, vouchers are extended to ensure that customers' flights will take place at a later date, thus making sure that they will still get the most out of their experience.

Virgin Balloon Flights celebrated their 25th anniversary in 2019, and they have been helping people to make their airborne dreams come true throughout those years. This has included romantic flights for couples, people celebrating special occasions such as wedding anniversaries, and in 2015 they welcomed their oldest passenger in the form of a 100-year-old customer who had always wanted to realise her lifelong dream of travelling in a hot air balloon.

Perthshire has a well-deserved reputation for being home to some of the most beautiful countryside in Scotland. A hot air balloon flight is the perfect way to see the city of Perth and its surroundings in the most unique circumstances imaginable. It really is an experience that participants will never forget.

Chapter Six

The Historical Southern Boundary

THE Historical Southern Boundary of Heart 200 takes visitors to some of the most remarkable places the route has to offer. Centuries of Scottish history are in evidence here, from the World War II-era Cultybraggan Prisoner of War Camp in Comrie to incredible Loch Leven – where Mary, Queen of Scots was once imprisoned on the remote Castle Island. From the ancient Dupplin Cross to the world-famous Gleneagles Hotel, this length of the Heart 200 route invites you to engage with a vast expanse of history from the Romans through to Queen Victoria and beyond.

But like the rest of the journey, there is even more to look forward to than culture and heritage. There are distilleries and market towns offering a whole range of unusual and often unexpected gift ideas, outdoor activities to suit nature enthusiasts, and of course plenty of sporting pursuits – including one of the most famous of all Scottish pastimes, a round of golf, in some of the most amazing scenery you can imagine!

Kinross

An important and culturally significant burgh in Perth and Kinross County, Kinross (from the Gaelic *Ceann Rois*, or 'Wood End') is the traditional county town of the historic county of Kinross-shire and a very popular destination for tourists given its central location between Glasgow, Stirling, Perth, St Andrews and Edinburgh. At one point, no less than three independent railway companies owned a terminus in Kinross due to the town's regional importance. In the modern day, it is just as well-

known for its vibrant arts, leisure and culture scene as it is for its major historical consequence.

Located on the shores of Loch Leven, Kinross boasts no shortage of sporting and leisure activities – not least the town's popular sports centre, Live Active Loch Leven (*www.liveactive.co.uk/ Venues/live-active-loch-leven*), situated in Lathro Lane. With a range of personal fitness programmes and activities, including a swimming pool and indoor sporting pursuits, the centre has much to offer its visitors. For those who prefer the great outdoors, the Loch Leven Heritage Trail initiative (*www.pkct.org/loch-leven-heritage-trail*) presents a unique path spanning 13 miles (21km) of beautiful countryside around the loch's shoreline, which is perfect for walkers and cyclists of all levels of experience. This walk provides the perfect balance of natural beauty and cultural history, taking in not only Kinross but also many of its surrounding towns and villages including Milnathort, Kinnesswood and Scotlandwell.

Historical sites in the area, all of which are well worth checking out, include the striking, historic Orwell Parish Church and graveyards (*www.scotlandschurchestrust.org.uk/church/orwell-church-milnathort*) in North Street, Milnathort, which lie on the Loch Leven Heritage Trail. Constructed in 1729, the church is steeped in history and its interior contains beautiful embroidered banners which were crafted by members of its congregation. It is now a Category A listed building. Nearby, between Milnathort and Balgedie, the Standing Stones of Orwell (*www.kinross.cc/ milnathort/stones.htm*) form an ancient megalithic circle dating back as far as 2000BC.

The imposing ruins of stately Burleigh Castle (*www.historicenvironment.scot/visit-a-place/ places/burleigh-castle/*) can be found to the east of Milnathort, on Burleigh Road. Open during the summer months, between April and September, this three-storey tower house was the seat of the Balfour family for around 250 years. It is thought to

have been built between the late 15th and early 16th centuries, then greatly expanded near the end of the 16th century. Its remarkable Jacobean architecture is explained by information boards which detail the building's significance. The nearby Orwell War Memorial and Park (*www.warmemorials-online.org.uk/memorial/130759*) in Milnathort's South Street commemorates the fallen soldiers and officers of both World Wars; an elegant sandstone pillar first unveiled in November 1921, the memorial is surrounded by a peaceful and well-tended park area where visitors can pay their respects.

To the north of Loch Leven, the impressive Balvaird Castle (*www.historicenvironment.scot/visit-a-place/places/balvaird-castle/*) was the home of the Murrays of Balvaird, who are thought to have constructed the property at the end of the 15th century, extending it in the 16th century and eventually departing in 1658. Today, it retains many notable features including a walled garden and park, as well as expansive inner and outer courtyards.

With its stunning gardens, the exquisite Kinross House Estate (*www.kinrosshouse.com*) is a prime example of a 17th century rural mansion house. The estate offers a wide variety of events including dinner parties in their dining room, banquets for up to 90 people in the Grand Salon, and marquee events in their garden for groups of up to 450 individuals. The Coach House on the estate (which, having been constructed in 1680, is actually older than Kinross House itself) has become a

sought-after destination for day spa treatments and hydrotherapy, while its baronial dining hall can seat up to 60 guests. The estate prides itself on its eclectic, high-quality range of events for guests throughout the year, which include casino nights, murder mystery evenings, Highland dance, pipe bands, bands, whisky tastings, and much more besides.

While there are many areas of historical interest in Kinross, principal among them is Loch Leven Castle (*www.historicenvironment.scot/visit-a-place/places/lochleven-castle/*). Built on an island in the loch during the 14th century, the castle has huge historical significance on account of its links to King Robert the Bruce and Robert the High Stewart (1316-90) – the latter being held captive within its walls in 1369, two years before being crowned King of Scots in 1371. However, Loch Leven Castle is likely to always be remembered most keenly as the site of Mary, Queen of Scots' abdication of the throne of Scotland in favour of her then infant son, King James VI, in 1568. The castle's four-storey tower remains a commanding structure amidst beautiful surroundings. Boat trips to

the island, which take approximately ten minutes in either direction, are usually made a number of times a day on a shuttle basis between April and October; it is recommended that anyone who is interested in paying a visit to the castle should check availability in advance.

Nature enthusiasts won't want to overlook the chance of a visit to the RSPB Scotland Loch Leven Nature Reserve (*www.rspb.org.uk/reserves-and-events/reserves-a-z/loch-leven/*) on the loch's southern shore, where beautiful woodland and wetlands are home to birds, animals and fish of many varieties. Hides and trails are available for those seeking to view the amazing wildlife in their natural habitat. In particular, ospreys can often be seen in the summer, while pink-footed geese are a regular feature during the autumn months. Walking destinations around the area include hill walks to Kilmagad Wood and a ramble around Loch Fitty, as well as trails within the stunning environs of

Loch Leven National Nature Reserve itself – a zone which encircles the entire loch.

Due to its breathtaking natural beauty, Loch Leven has become a favourite destination of film-makers over the years. Michael Caton-Jones's 1995 Academy Award-nominated *Rob Roy*, a retelling of the life of outlaw and folk hero Rob Roy Mac-Gregor which featured Liam Neeson in the title role, included location filming at Loch Leven as well as at Drummond Castle near Crieff. One of the most famous films ever to feature Scotland, Mel Gibson's 1995 epic *Braveheart* – which won the Academy Award for Best Picture – starred Gibson himself as Sir William Wallace, and included unforgettable location filming which took place around Loch Leven. Decades earlier, Hollywood legend Kirk Douglas starred in tongue-in-cheek 1971 espionage drama *Catch Me a Spy*, directed by Dick Clement, which involved a Cold War-era smuggler of microfilm involved in a plot to traffic Russian secrets back to the West. It too was to feature location filming on the exquisite shores of the loch.

Anyone seeking a more modern visitor experience may prefer to visit Loch Leven Brewery (*www.lochleven.beer*) at the Muirs, Kinross – a local company with highly knowledgeable staff and an on-site distillery which offers beer-tasting (along with many other beverages) within in a warm and friendly environment. Their Great Scots range of beers are named in honour of historical figures from Scotland's past, including Outlaw King (Robert the Bruce), Shining Knight (Andrew Carnegie), Warrior Queen (Mary, Queen of Scots) and King Slayer (Gabriel de Montgomery). The brewery also offers private events and room hire for special occasions. For those seeking an alternative retail experience in Kinross, Cashmere at Loch Leven (*www.cashmereatlochleven.com*) at Loch Leven Mills, based at the end of the High Street, is the perfect location for male and female cashmere garments and accessories, as well as clothing from other popular brands, gifts and jewellery. A coffee shop is also on the premises.

In recent years, Kinross has made a name for itself as a terrific venue for live music. Mundell Music (*www.mundellmusic.com*) has been a promoter of live gigs in Scotland for over two decades, and specialises in arranging intimate performances with a maximum audience of 120 people. They cover a vast array of different music genres, attracting local artists and touring bands both new and long established. They have become increasingly well-known for 'Backstage at the Green', a music venue at Kinross's Green Hotel (*www.green-hotel.com*) which hosts music shows throughout the year – as well as a first-rate collection of rock 'n' roll memorabilia. Why not check ahead of your visit and see what acts will be performing while you're in the town? Advance booking is highly recommended.

Glendevon and Gleneagles
A scenic village popular with visitors making the trip between Kinross and Gleneagles, the tranquil settlement of Glendevon is a peaceful place situated

amidst some lovely scenery. It has become a well-liked stopping point for walkers and cyclists in the area, with particular admiration amongst ramblers for the eye-catching, popular Glen Sherup circular route (*www.woodlandtrust.org.uk/visiting-woods/woods/glen-sherup*) – a pleasant woodland walk with some jaw-dropping views from the summit of the nearby hills. This extensive woodland features varied wildlife including red squirrels and pine martens, with a variety of environments ranging from moorland to grassland. A waymarked walk is in place for visitors to the area.

Another popular destination is the Glen Sherup Fishery (*www.glensherup-fishery.co.uk*), a trout loch on beautiful unspoilt waters spanning 29 acres which is the perfect place for those seeking to spend some time off the beaten track. The area is especially well-known for its rainbow trout and brown trout. Prices and terms of hire are available on the company's website, and it is advised to check ahead of time if you want to pay a visit.

Situated near the speciality luxury lodgings of the village's well-appointed Glendevon Country Park (*www.ariaresorthomes.co.uk/dumfries-galloway-and-perthshire/glendevon-country-park/*) lies one of the area's most unique attractions: the exquisitely-maintained Japanese Garden at Cowden (*www.cowdengarden.com*), between Glendevon and Dollar. This historic garden was the brainchild of Isabella 'Ella' Christie (1861-1949), the far-travelled owner of Cowden Castle, and her high regard for the culture and traditions of the Far East inspired her to employ the talents of Japanese horticulturalist Taki Handa to create *Sha Raku En*, which translates as 'the place of pleasure and delight'. The seven-acre grounds bring an authentic touch of Japan to Clackmannanshire, nestled in the Ochil Hills, and include a stroll garden, a pond and island garden, and a tea-house garden.

Cowden Castle was demolished in 1952, and the Japanese Garden was destroyed by vandals in 1963. However, Professor Masao Fukuhara of the Osaka University of Arts was appointed in 2013 to restore the gardens, and – as a high-profile campaign of media coverage has described – the grounds are being painstakingly renovated in order to reflect their original glory. There is also a network of restored woodland walks around the area which demonstrate the natural beauty of the grounds to its fullest extent. For details of events and opening times, please consult the Cowden Garden website.

Glen Eagles (or, more commonly, 'Gleneagles') is the name given to the valley which connects with Glen Devon to form a natural corridor through the Ochil Hills. Its name derives from the Gaelic *Gleann Eaglais*, meaning literally 'the Glen of the Church', signifying the chapel and well of the 6th century evangelist St Mungo (now the Patron Saint of Glasgow) situated within the Gleneagles Estate, owned by the Haldane Clan.

A location that is immediately synonymous with its most famous attraction, the Perthshire village of Gleneagles is home to the luxury Gleneagles Hotel (*www.gleneagles.com*) – an establishment which has been offering the height of sumptuous accommodation since it first opened in 1924. Constructed by the Caledonian Railway Company (which was later bought over by the London, Midland and Scottish Railway), the hotel is famous for being served by its own dedicated railway branch line – Gleneagles Railway Station, which is situated nearby – and is now universally recognised as being one of the leading hotels in the world.

A Category B listed building since 1980, Gleneagles is famed for its three golf courses (the King's Course, Queen's Course and PGA Centenary Course) as well as its 9-hole course (the PGA National Academy Course), and has been the location of several major international golf tournaments including the Ryder Cup, the Solheim Cup, the Women's British Open, the Scottish Open and the European Golf Team Championships. The grounds are also home to the British School of Falconry, while the hotel has hosted numerous major global conferences including – perhaps most famously – the 31st international G8 Summit in July 2005, which was attended by such political luminaries as Prime Minister Tony Blair, U.S. President George W. Bush and German Chancellor Gerhard Schröder. The Bilderberg Group met at the hotel in April 1986, while the building also lends its name to the Gleneagles Agreement of 1977 approved by the Commonwealth of Nations.

Gleneagles Hotel has won a large number of major awards over the years, both for its hospitality and its status as one of the planet's most prominent golf resorts. These have included Scotland's Best Hotel at the Today's Golfer Travel Awards on four separate occasions, and Best Golf Resort in the World by Ultratravel Magazine on six occasions to date. It has the distinction of having held five Red AA Stars since 1986. However, Gleneagles is so much more than a golfer's paradise; the hotel offers just about every possible kind of amenity to ensure that visitors enjoy their stay.

The facilities at Gleneagles Hotel are as celebrated as they are multifarious. Popular activities amongst guests include falconry, shooting, tennis, cycling, archery, fishing, horse riding and off-road driving. With 850 acres of grounds, time spent in the great outdoors at Gleneagles is always an experience to remember. The hotel boasts its own range of fine foods, including luxury Gleneagles & Co. chocolate, and the health and beauty options on offer are also hugely sought-after – whether at the

Spa, the Health Club or the Bob and Cloche: the hotel's dedicated hair and beauty lodge. There are facilities specially intended for younger visitors, meeting and function rooms, extensive wedding services, and so much more besides. With its impeccably-maintained grounds, renowned customer service, well-stocked fitness centre and array of fine dining options, a visit to Gleneagles will almost certainly be among the highlights of your Heart 200 travels.

Gleneagles has also made an indelible mark upon popular culture over the years. The hotel was the location of Scotland's first outside broadcast (the production of a radio programme from a remote broadcast studio) on 7 June 1924, in a presentation featuring a performance by the legendary dance band leader Henry Hall CBE (1898-1989). One of the most controversial TV thrillers of the 1980s, *Edge of Darkness*, was broadcast by the BBC in 1985. Filming took place at Gleneagles, including at the magnificent grounds of Gleneagles Hotel. This multiple BAFTA-winning political miniseries,

directed by Martin Campbell, was highly topical at the time and starred Bob Peck and Joe Don Baker. Some time later, novelist Ian Rankin used the hotel – and specifically the 2005 G8 Summit – as one of the settings for his acclaimed Inspector Rebus novel *The Naming of the Dead* (2006).

Auchterarder and Dunning

Known locally as the 'lang toun' ('long town') on account of its one-and-a-half mile long high street, Auchterarder is only a short drive away from Gleneagles Hotel and is a truly charming place with plenty to see and do. From its independent shops to its diverse eateries, the town is popular with tourists and is regularly visited by guests staying at Gleneagles.

References to the town date back as far as the 13th century, and though it was destroyed by the Earl of Mar during the Jacobite uprising in 1716 it was rebuilt thereafter and continued to be regarded as one of the leading towns in the area

due to its industrial significance, particularly its weaving and textile manufacturing. The town became a burgh in 1892.

History aficionados will no doubt be interested to view the ruins of ancient Auchterarder Castle (*www.ancientmonuments.uk/125638-auchterarder-castle-strathallan-ward*) in the town's Castleton area, once used by King Malcolm Canmore (c.1031-93) for hunting in the 11th century, though only fragments remain of this once-grand building remain today. Also of historical significance is Tullibardine Chapel (*www.historicenvironment.scot/visit-a-place/places/tullibardine-chapel*), a 16th century place of worship located to the north-west of Auchterarder. Based in peaceful surroundings, this church building is noteworthy in that it persisted through the Reformation with few changes, and features a roof that dates back to the late medieval period.

Visitors looking for more strenuous outdoor activities can find out about the best ways to cycle around this picturesque area by checking in with Synergy Cycles (*www.synergycycles.cc*) in Auchterarder's High Street for information about how to make the most of their time in the area. The company is widely considered to be among Scotland's foremost road and electric bicycle shops, with accessories to suit novices and advanced cyclists alike. Fans of more extreme sports may prefer to seek out the acclaimed Skydive Strathallan (*www.skydivestrathallan.co.uk*), which has been offering its visitors memorable skydiving experiences since 1960. This breathtaking pastime, carried out safely under the supervision of the company's highly-trained professionals, is hugely popular, and every year they welcome around 1500 people to offer training on their first solo or tandem parachute jump – as well as regular members who enjoy the experience more frequently. Their website contains extensive information about the services that the company provides, including details about how to organise charity parachute jumps.

For those who prefer to stay on solid ground, the Tullibardine Distillery (*www.tullibardine.com*) based in nearby Blackford is on hand to reveal the art of producing their prized, hand-crafted single malt Scotch whisky. Based in the village's Stirling Street, the distillery has a long and fascinating history which dates back as far as 1488, when King James IV (1473-1513) purchased beer from a local brewery in the area and later granted the business a Royal Charter in 1503. Many centuries later, in 1947, that historic brewery was conscientiously converted into the Tullibardine Distillery by William Delmé-Evans (1920-2003), which was perfectly situated to make the most of the pure water supply to create a truly distinctive whisky. The story of the distillery, and its products, is told in detail at the on-site visitor centre, where this family-owned business explains the continued success of their whisky not just in Scotland, but all around the world. With a bottling plant on the premises, the entire process of whisky creation – from distillation and maturing to bottling – all takes place in the one location. Why not find out more about the practice by paying them a visit?

The town is also home to the historic, welcoming and well-maintained Auchterarder Golf Club (*www.auchterardergolf.co.uk*) in Orchil Road, which greets visitors all the year round. The Club was founded in 1892, and its 9-hole course was developed by Ben Sayers (1856-1924) in 1913 – though it was significantly expanded in the 1970s, and the current 18-hole course was opened in 1979. Today the Club is an enduringly sought-after destination for golfers, and its clubhouse has been extended on a number of occasions over recent years in order to meet increasing demand. Visitors' information is available on their website, including additional facilities such as their bar, lounge and dining room areas.

Many famous people have been born in Auchterarder over the decades, including novelist James Kennaway (1928-68), author of *Tunes of Glory* (1956); wartime Spitfire pilot Sandy Gunn (1919-44), who participated in 'The Great Escape'; crystallographer Professor John Monteath Robertson FRSE (1900-89); The New Seekers singer Eve Graham (1943-); newspaper editor John Gordon (1890-1974); and religious writer the Rev. Dr Robert Nisbet FRSE (1814-74).

A few miles to the east of Auchterarder, the attractive village of Dunning has a very long history; in its vicinity the Iron Age fort of Dun Knock and the Kincladie Roman camp from the 1st century were once situated, while legends state that the 6th century Saint Serf slayed a dragon while visiting the area. That historical figure lends his name to St Serf's Church (*www.historicenvironment.scot/visit-a-place/places/st-serfs-church-and-dupplin-cross*), in Tron Square, which is thought to date from approximately 1200AD and around which the modern village was formed. Surrounded by a cemetery with gravestones dating back as far as the early 17th century, the church was extensively remodelled in the 19th century and contains wonderful stained glass created by the famous firm of Ballantyne and Son. Its preserved Romanesque architecture is also very much in evidence. The church continued to be an active place of worship until 1972, but now is maintained by Historic Environment Scotland which has continued to ensure that it is available for public viewing seasonally between April and September. The church was used as a filming location in Gavin Millar's film *Complicity* (2000), a cinematic adaptation of Iain Banks's critically-acclaimed 1993 novel of the same name.

St Serf's Church is the location of the extraordinary Dupplin Cross (*www.undiscovered-scotland.co.uk/dunning/stserfs/*), a 9th century Pictish stone carving which was relocated from an exterior location on a hill at Forteviot (around three miles to the north-east of Dunning) in 1999, put through a meticulous conservation process, and

then carefully placed in the church in order to better preserve it for future generations. Previously situated next to the site of a Pictish royal palace, the stone is intricately carved and highly decorated, its design featuring characters from Biblical and Ecclesiastical history. Within the church, there is significant information about the cross and its history, as well as interpretation of its elaborate decoration.

Also situated near St Serf's Church is an ornamental fountain at the centre of Dunning which was donated to the village in 1874 by Alexander Martin (1801-1874), a highly successful confectioner. Martin had lived in Dunning prior to moving to St John in the Canadian province of New Brunswick in 1840, where his business proved highly profitable. The fountain is constructed in the medieval style and contains a number of ornate stone carvings, including animal figures.

Like nearby Auchterarder, Dunning was destroyed by burning during the Jacobite Rebellion in 1716, and a thorn tree (which has been replaced a number of times over the century) was planted in Thorn Tree Square – on the Yetts o' Muckhart Road – in commemoration of this devastating historical event.

While Dunning has a population estimated at only 1,000 residents, it has been the birthplace of numerous noteworthy figures including botanist Professor James Robert Mathews FRSE FLS (1889-1978) and classicist Sir John Mackay Thomson FRSE (1887-1974). The Very Rev. Professor James Paton Gloag (1823-1906), born in Perth, was appointed Dunning's Minister from 1848 to 1857, and was later to be named Moderator of the General Assembly of the Church of Scotland in 1889. Today, the industrious Dunning Community Trust (*www.dunning-community-trust.org.uk*) continues to develop new amenities for the village, which include a recreation area which comprises a tennis court, football pitch and 9-hole golf course. With environmental conservation at the heart of their enterprise, the trust has garnered particular praise for its promotion of the historic Kincladie Wood and beautiful Dunning Glen (both located in close proximity to the village), as well as the protection of their diverse ecology.

Another popular Dunning attraction is Broadslap Fruit Farm (*www.broadslapfruit-farm.co.uk*), a shop and café located close to the village. Open seasonally between spring and autumn, the farm is renowned not just for its range of vegetables and soft fruits (not least their fabulous raspberries), but also their delicatessen and range of events taking place at different points of the year. Their shop not only sells locally-grown soft fruits (including strawberries, blackcurrants, brambles, gooseberries and redcurrants), but also potatoes, meat, poultry and game. Their fine Perthshire produce is also available from their well-regarded café, which serves snacks and meals from the traditional to the contemporary. Check ahead on their website for details of availability.

A short drive to the north of Dunning, in the village of Methven, the Strathearn Distillery (*www.strathearndistillery.com*) at Bachilton Farm Steading is billed as Scotland's original craft spirits distillery, founded by Tony Reeman-Clark in 2013. Originally producing whisky and gin, the company now also distils rum, and their staff prides themselves on bringing new and innovative craft spirits

to the public. Members of the distillery's private Cask Club have the opportunity to visit the distillery – strictly by prior appointment only – and see first-hand how Strathearn Single Malt is made. This award-winning distillery's products are available far and wide, including their famous Highland Oaked gin, Heather Rose gin and, of course, their much-praised Strathearn Single Malt whisky.

Muthill

The attractive village of Muthill is a must-see destination for anyone with an interest in Scottish history. It was once a significant centre of religious activity for the area, and at one point was the location of a monastery for the Celí Dé (or 'Culdees', meaning 'Spouses of God') community during the Middle Ages. The medieval church at Muthill was also the seat of the Bishops of Strathearn until the construction of Dunblane Cathedral. Like a number of other settlements in the area, Muthill was

destroyed by fire in 1716 during the Jacobite Rebellion, but was rebuilt a few decades later.

Muthill contains a large number of listed buildings, but has become particularly well-known for its historic religious structures. These include the well-known sight of Muthill Parish Church (*www.muthillparishchurch.co.uk*) on Station Road, which was completed in 1828 by famed architect James Gillespie Graham (1776-1855). Graham was responsible for the design of innumerable prominent churches throughout Scotland and beyond, including the Tolbooth Kirk in Edinburgh, Falkirk Parish Church and Cambusnethan Priory. Muthill Parish Church remains a thriving worship community, and services take place there every Sunday – as well as numerous community-oriented amenities which operate throughout the week. Situated nearby, also on Station Road, St James Episcopal Church (*www.scotland-anglican.org/church/st-james-muthill*) was built in 1836 and is of considerable interest to Scottish historians, not least as it was designed by architects Richard (1792-1857) and Robert Dickson (c.1794-1865), who are most widely recognised for their design of the spire on Edinburgh's Tron Kirk in the Royal Mile. It also remains a functioning place of worship with an active congregation and range of services which work for the benefit of the local community.

The extensive ruins of the medieval Muthill Old Church (*www.historicenvironment.scot/visit-a-place/places/muthill-old-church-and-tower/*), also located in the village's Station Road, date back to

the 12th century. Its tower is thought to have been free-standing originally, with the church building being extended in the 15th century. While the church itself has lost its roof in the intervening period, the Romanesque tower remains intact. Further along Station Road, Visitors can find out more about the fascinating and often surprising history of the community at Muthill Village Museum (*www.culture24.org.uk/am16425*), based near the old churchyard. With many artefacts on display, here you can learn more about this ancient village's heritage as an important religious hub and hear about how its name may derive from 'Moot Hill': a place of judgement.

For those seeking a moment of peace and contemplation, Muthill has an attractive and neatly-maintained village green which is bordered by its War Memorial (*www.warmemorialsonline.org.uk/memorial/166848/*) on the junction of Thornhill Street and Willoughby Street. Other activities in

the area include the well-regarded Muthill Golf Club (*www.muthillgolfclub.co.uk*), first formed in 1911 but – due to its grounds being requisitioned for agricultural purposes during the First World War – temporarily closed and not reconstituted until 1934. Officially reopened in May 1935, the Club has grown and developed over the decades, with a redesigned course and extended clubhouse opening in 1977. Muthill Golf Club still extends an amiable welcome to visiting players today; check their website for details of green fees and other information prior to your trip.

The captivating Strathearn Wool Studio (*www.strathearnwooltryst.weebly.com*), operated by Strathearn Fleece and Fibre, is a working sheep farm with much to share about the process of how wool is made, from herding the flock through to shearing and dying the wool. Based at Culdees, just off the A822 near Muthill, the estate's 400 sheep produce the wool for a wide range of fleeces, rovings and yarns, which are available to buy on the premises. The studio also hosts an annual Wool Tryst, usually in September.

Noteworthy figures to be born in Muthill have included the Rev. John Barclay (1734-98), who founded the Berean Church; politician David Brydie Mitchell (1766-1837), three-time Governor of the American State of Georgia; and horticulturalist John Buchanan (1855-1896).

Crieff

The busy market town of Crieff (from the Gaelic *Craoibh*, or 'Tree') is home to attractions for just about everyone. As a settlement, it has a lengthy history – not least in terms of its mercantile significance, for it was once a vital centre of Scottish cattle trading. Drovers would come from far and wide, from the Highlands and even the Western Isles, to sell their cattle, and their number even included the notorious Rob Roy MacGregor. Though much of  the town was destroyed after Jacobites set fire to it in 1716 (a fate shared by numerous other settlements on the road of their retreat from the Battle of Sheriffmuir), Crieff quickly recovered in the following years and became an important industrial hub for textile manufacturing. From the 19th century onwards, the town became a popular tourist destination – a feature that it retains to this very day. Due to demand, a railway station opened in the town in 1856 and served Crieff for over a century until the Beeching cuts in 1964. The town's perennial popularity with visitors was cemented in 1868 with the establishment of the Crieff Hydropathic Establishment in Ferntower Road by Dr Henry Thomas Meikle (1834-1913). Now one of Scotland's leading spa resorts, Crieff Hydro Hotel (*www.crieffhydro.com*) today boasts over two hundred bedrooms and more than fifty self-catering properties, as well as many other facilities including conference rooms, a restaurant and Victorian dining room, and a huge range of leisure facilities for indoor and outdoor sports. These include gymnasium services, racquet sport courts, football pitches, horse-riding stables, swimming pools, a golf course and much more besides. Crieff Hydro is a Category B listed building, and the recipient of many awards including the Gold Green Tourism Award, Perthshire Chamber of Commerce Business of the Year, and numerous others.

A handy resource for new arrivals is Crieff Visitor Centre (*www.crieff.co.uk*) in Muthill Road, which provides not only information but also a well-stocked shop which sells gifts, fashion items and accessories, a restaurant and even a gardening shop. The centre is also home to an excellent exhibition focusing upon the Highland cattle drovers, presenting a valuable and entertaining look

at Crieff's place in Scottish history. The centre additionally features an outdoor play area for younger visitors, and offers numerous walks around the area suitable for guests of all age groups; ask the tourist information staff for more information.

Also based at the visitor centre is one of the town's most well-known attractions, the Caithness Glass showroom (*www.caithnessglass.co.uk*), where visitors can watch beautiful glassware being hand-crafted by experts, and (by appointment only) even take part in glass-painting and paperweight-crafting sessions themselves under the supervision of an experienced expert. Numerous celebrities and public figures have tried their hand at crafting glass on the premises; don't forget to have a look at the showroom's photographic hall of fame to see who has enjoyed a visit before you! Caithness Glass has been handcrafting glassware since 1961, and their products are prized the world over. Their retail shop area deals in a variety of intricately-designed ornaments and paperweights – many of them

personalised for special occasions or limited editions. A wide range of Caithness products, as well as other glassware and crystal items, are available to buy from the showroom.

No visit to Crieff would be complete without a visit to the amazing Nutcracker Christmas Shop (*www.nutcrackerchristmasshop.co.uk*) – one of the largest stores of its type in the UK. Based in Muthill Road, Christmas decorations and other festively-themed items are available to buy all the year round in this fantastic celebration of all things yuletide. They have a vast array of scented candles and festive fragrances, Christmas stockings, tree decorations, Santa Claus ornaments, Nativity scenes and traditional German wooden nutcrackers. The shop is set up in the style of a traditional European village at Christmas, with a central Christmas tree and numerous 'houses' arranged around the village square – each of them with a different theme and related products within, just waiting for your perusal. The Nutcracker Christmas Shop is a

family-run business which was founded by Robert Newman in 2001. They now have a number of shops in other towns throughout the UK, though the Crieff Christmas Village is their largest. The shop is open seven days a week, and a virtual tour is available on the company's website.

One of Crieff's premier visitor attractions is the Famous Grouse Experience at the Glenturret Distillery (*www.theglenturret.com*), Scotland's oldest working whisky distillery. Established by

Hugh and John Drummond in 1775 as a single malt distillery, it has been drawing the pure waters of Turret Burn for well over two centuries to create one of Scotland's best-loved brands of whisky. Located at The Hosh, near Crieff, the distillery has maintained the long-held traditions that have made it one of the country's most celebrated producers of whisky, while providing a thoroughly modern visitor experience. As well as tours, whisky tasting is available, as is a bar, restaurant, café, and a shop area. Anyone seeking to buy a whisky-themed gift for true aficionados is bound to find something of interest at the distillery. Their website features a 360° virtual tour of the premises, giving you a taste of the Glenturret experience even before you visit. There is also the Guild of Glenturret membership programme, which allows access to various exclusives and some very welcome members' benefits.

The Glenturret Distillery is home to one of the last open-top Mash Tuns in Scottish whisky production, and it currently uses the last hand-operated Mash Tun of its

kind in the industry. The distillery also has one of the longest fermentation times in Scotch whisky production, with an average time of around 90-100 hours (as opposed to the industry average of 48-56 hours). However, the distillery has another

claim to fame in that it was recognised as holding a very unexpected Guinness World Record. From 1963 through to 1987, the distillery's still house was occupied by Towser the cat, a vigilant feline who managed to catch some 28,899 mice in her long and distinguished career on the premises. Following her death in March 1987, she was officially recognised as the World's Greatest Mouser, with this title being formally documented by the Guinness Book of Records. There is now a statue of Towser on the distillery grounds, which is visited by tourists from all over the world each year. Some even think that Towser's amazing success as a mouser came down to the belief that she had a 'tiny wee dram' of whisky in her milk every night!

The Glenturret Distillery has been the recipient of many awards, including the Whisky Magazine's Icons of Whisky Awards, International Spirits Challenge Awards and the Association of Scottish Visitor Attractions Awards, and has been rated a five star visitor attraction by the Scottish Tourist Board. With a friendly welcome, knowledgeable staff and plenty to interest whisky enthusiasts and history buffs alike, a visit to their premises is highly recommended. Be sure to consult their website for a look at some of the many visitor experiences that they offer.

For a slightly different kind of retail experience, why not consider paying a visit to the celebrated Gordon and Durward Sweet Shop (*www.scottishsweets.co.uk*) on Crieff's West High Street? Since 1925, the company has been supplying the public with the finest confectionery, including fudge, macaroon, marzipan, butter tablet, coconut ice and truffles, along with various gift boxes perfect for anyone with a sweet tooth. But Gordon and Durward isn't just any confectioner: it is the originator of the famous 'sugar mice', which are now loved the world over. They remain renowned not just for the immaculate quality of their products, but also the wide range of sweets that they offer their customers throughout the year. The company was even once named the Number 1 Best Sweet Shop in Scotland by *The Scotsman* newspaper – an achievement not to be sniffed at!

Anyone with an interest in history will be keen to seek out the historic Library of Innerpeffray (*www.innerpeffraylibrary.co.uk*), the oldest lending library in Scotland. Based in the village of Innerpeffray (approximately four miles south-east of Crieff), the library was founded in 1680 by Lord David Drummond (1610-92) in the attic of the village's St Mary's Chapel, though the growing collection of books soon necessitated that the collection expanded to a building constructed nearby in the kirkyard. The Rev. Robert Hay Drummond (1711-76), later Archbishop of York, inherited the estate in 1739 and commissioned the construction of a custom-built library and reading room, designed by architect Charles Freebairn (?-c.1781). The collection of books was moved to the new structure in 1762, which is now a Category A listed building. Though the lending of the library's books to the public was ended in 1968, the building is still open to visitors between spring and autumn, and remains a book-lover's paradise. The library contains a treasure trove of rare publications, among them a Bible belonging to the Marquis of Montrose (1633), a first edition copy of John Knox's *Historie of the Reformation* (1644), early editions of Robert Burns's legendary *Poems, Chiefly in the Scottish Dialect* (1787-88), and innumerable other publications – some of them dating back as far as the 16th century. The library also has a shop with souvenirs guaranteed to suit all bibilophiles: there are badges, bookmarks, bags, cushions, notebooks and plenty of other exclusive merchandise on offer, along with the chance to 'befriend a book': ask a staff member for more details. Because of the seasonal opening hours, checking the website ahead of time to ensure availability is recommended before your trip to the library.

Explorers in the Crieff area will be spoiled for choice, as there are many areas of interest that are based in and around the town. Foremost among these destinations is the stunning Drummond Castle Gardens (*www.drummondcastlegardens.co.uk*), which is widely considered one of the finest formal gardens in all of Europe. Drummond Gardens are located two miles south of Crieff, and featured in season 2 of *Outlander*, where they portrayed the gardens of the Palace of Versailles. They also featured in Michael Caton-Jones's film *Rob Roy* (1995). Visitors will soon discover why the gardens are so beloved of film-makers on their arrival. First established by John Drummond (1588-1662), 2nd Earl of Perth, in the 1630s, the gardens were extensively redesigned and expanded in the 19th century and include a copper beech tree planted by Queen Victoria when she visited in 1842. A major replanting effort took place after World War II, and the gardens today are one of the most beautiful destinations in all of Perthshire. The gardens are open to the public from Easter until late summer; for details of admission fees and opening times, visit the website. Please note that the Category B listed Drummond Castle itself, which dates back to the 17th century, is not open to the public.

Visitors are sure to enjoy the wide open spaces of Macrosty Park (*www.pkc.gov.uk/article/15315/MacRosty-Park-in-Crieff*), just off the A85, which is the perfect place for families, offering pic-nic areas, a café, a Victorian-era bandstand, and plenty of well-maintained parkland. Other local attractions include the Category B listed stone four-arch Crieff Bridge (*www.sabre-roads-.org.uk/wiki/index.php?title=Crieff_Bridge*) over the River Earn, the town's Diamond Jubilee Fountain (*www.inspirock.com/united-kingdom/crieff/diamond-jubilee-fountain-a9482561469*) which is located between Rosslyn Street and Gower Street, and Buchanty Spout (*www.holidayscotland.org.uk/salmon-leaping-perthshire*) on the River Almond – where, if you are very lucky, you might spot a salmon leaping through the water on its way up-stream.

A popular walking destination from Crieff is the Loch Turret reservoir (*www.scottish-places.info/features/featurefirst2641.html*), around five miles north-west of Crieff, which opened in 1964 and comprises an area of around 378 hectares. Other well-known routes include the delightful Lady Mary's Walk (*www.visitscotland.com/info/*

towns-villages/lady-marys-walk-p249261) along the banks of the River Earn, which is perfect for nature lovers. The nearby village of Fowlis Wester (*www.ancient-scotland.co.uk/site/86*) is famed for its many ancient sites, not least its stone circles, and is sure to fascinate any admirers of the Neolithic.

For golfing visitors, the highly-rated Crieff Golf Club (*www.crieffgolf.co.uk*) on Perth Road was founded in 1891 and featured a 9-hole course designed by Old Tom Morris. Built on what had, at one time, been the expansive grounds of Ferntower House, the club has extended over the years and now comprises of the Ferntower and Dornock courses. With an excellent clubhouse and pro shop, visitors will enjoy a memorable golfing experience. Please check the website ahead of your trip for the latest details on green fees and booking tee time.

Those seeking more energetic pursuits will want to visit Action Glen (*crieff.actionglen.com*), a well-liked adventure centre at Ferntower Road which offers a wide variety of activities including quad-biking, treetop adventures and Segway treks. Based on a 900 acre estate, there is an off-road sand and gravel quarry, a golf course – and, for those seeking to recover from their rigorous workout, a restaurant and bar!

The town is also host to Crieff Highland Gathering (*www.crieffhighlandgathering.com*), which takes place on an annual basis and invites spectators to watch competitors in the gruelling Highland Games as well as offering live music and other activities. Taking place in late summer at Market Park, a full programme of events take place including highland dancing, a tug o' war and bagpiping performances.

Many famous people have been born in Crieff, including international rugby player Simon Taylor (1979-); actor Denis Lawson (1947-) and his nephew, film star Ewan McGregor (1971-); David Jacks (1822-1909), the first businessperson to popularise Monterey Jack cheese; politicians Gavin Strang (1943-) and Rory Stewart (1973-); and footballer Jackie Dewar (1923-2011). The town also has an unlikely claim to literary fame in that the infamous Scottish poet William Topaz McGonagall (1825-1902) composed a poem in its honour, entitled simply *Beautiful Crieff* (1899).

Comrie

Comrie is known throughout Scotland as the 'shaky toun', due to the fact that statistically it experiences more tremors than any other town in the

UK on account of it being located on the Highland Boundary fault line. This unique part of Comrie's heritage is immortalised in the story of the town's distinctive Earthquake House (*www.undiscovered-scotland.co.uk/comrie/earthquakehouse/*), situated in a nearby field to detect seismic activity. The house (really a sort of stone-built cabin) is reachable from a minor road from the A85 to the west of Comrie. While it cannot be entered by visitors, be sure to check out the adjacent information board to learn the fascinating story of the town's seismograph. The building was constructed in 1874, and restored in 1988 with modern sensor equipment.

Comrie has been occupied since prehistoric times, and numerous archaeological sites have suggested later habitation by Picts and Celts. The Roman Empire established a fort near the current settlement in 79AD, and – centuries later – King James V (1512-42) became a regular visitor due to annual deer-hunting trips he undertook there. The town flourished on account of cattle trading and weaving, and during the Victorian era it became a very popular tourist destination. A railway station was established in the town in 1893, and continued to serve the area until it was closed in 1964 (due to the Beeching cuts). It retains its attractive appearance and active community spirit today, and is also noteworthy for its architecture; Charles Rennie Mackintosh (1868-1928) redesigned one of the shops in the town's main street – the Brough and Macpherson Shop – recognisable by its distinguishing corner turret, in 1903, and there are numerous buildings throughout Comrie which indicate the town's lengthy history as a settlement. These include many traditional cottages as well as grander Victorian and Edwardian structures.

The visual centrepiece of Comrie town centre is widely considered to be its White Church (*www.comriewhitechurch.co.uk*) in Dunira Street, now the Comrie Community Centre. Constructed as a church in 1805, the building eventually became a community centre in 1965. With support from the Millennium Commission and other fundraisers, the centre was extensively refurbished in 2000. It is a Category A listed building which is situated on the bank of the River Earn, and is a striking sight in all seasons. With three halls of different sizes, including the Earn Suite and the Lednock Hall, the centre is a popular venue for all kinds of occasions, and there are many regular social events held there including a parent and toddler group, a cinema club and film festival, a weekly lunch club, a quiz every month, an annual pantomime, a craft fair,

instruction in yoga, a dramatic arts group, and much more besides. With so many things going on there, it's always worth checking the latest news update on their website for a schedule of forthcoming events.

Nature lovers will no doubt be keen to visit the family-oriented Auchingarrich Wildlife Centre (*www.auchingarrich.co.uk*), located about a mile from Comrie town centre, with its wonderful assortment of animals – forty different species in all – ranging from Highland cows to llamas and emus. A wide range of activities are available for visitors, and the staff members are very well-informed and happy to help. There are pony rides, indoor and outdoor play, animal feeding, mini golf, a soft play barn, and even (seasonally only) the chance to visit a hatchery and handle tiny chicks, as well as other animals such as tortoises, rabbits and guinea pigs. A visit to the centre really is a dream come true for animal kingdom enthusiasts everywhere.

Those who prefer their open-air pursuits to be a little bit more energetic may prefer the thrills of Do It Outdoors (*www.comrie.org.uk/business-directory/6833/do-it-outdoors*), where traditional pastimes such as archery and axe-throwing are the order of the day. Many other activities are on offer, including bushcraft courses and instruction in fly-fishing, and the company – which also operates from nearby Auchterarder – has become a firm favourite for children's parties.

Anyone seeking to blend retail with an interest in art need look no further than the Riverside Garden Centre and Art Gallery (*www.comrie-perth-and-kinross.cylex-uk.co.uk/company/river-side-garden-centre-2377723.html*), where an array of plants and flowers can be purchased alongside a fine range of locally-sourced arts and crafts such as hand-carved wooden boxes, original artwork, jewellery and glassware.

Comrie is a hugely popular place amongst walkers, and for good reason – there is no shortage of picturesque destinations to suit everyone from beginners through to experienced hikers. The best-known places to visit in the area include the staggering Deil's Cauldron (*www.walkhighlands.co.uk/perthshire/deils-cauldron.shtml*), where walkers can see waters from the River Lednock cascading from a ravine surrounded by an impressive forested natural arena, with the option of ascending to the Melville Monument (*www.inspirock.com/united-kingdom/comrie/melville-monument-a1469124973*), a granite obelisk on Dùn Mòr hill overlooking the town which offers a breathtaking vista. This 72 foot-tall column is a memorial to Henry Dundas FRSE, 1st Viscount Melville (1742-1811), designed by architect James Gillespie Graham (1776-1855) in 1812. Other popular walking destinations include Glen Artney, an attractive glen and one-time royal deer forest; the Sput Rolla waterfall; the Dalgincross Bridge, constructed in 1904 by Sir William Arrol (1839-1913); and the Dundas Monument at the east end of the town. There is also the famously beautiful 'Circular Walk' around Glen Lednock (*www.gateway-to-the-scottish-highlands.com/Glen-Lednock.html*). Check during your visit for leaflets and information about the many walking routes around the town.

Established in 1891 at Laggan Braes, Comrie Golf Club (*www.comriegolf.co.uk*) is a 9-hole course that has been welcoming visitors for well over a century. With wonderful Perthshire scenery and delicious on-site catering at the clubhouse, the course is particularly well-known for its inventive-

ly-named course: it has holes with monikers such as 'Betty's Knowe', 'Happy Valley' and 'Johnnie's Corner'. For details of green fees and course layout, be sure to check the Club website.

Nobody with an interest in history will want to pass up the chance of a visit to one of Comrie's most unique and noteworthy places: Cultybraggan Camp (*www.comriedevelopmenttrust.org.uk/about-us/cultybraggan*). Located one mile south of Comrie, Cultybraggan was once a World War II prisoner of war camp (POW Camp 21) which has been preserved in astonishing condition near the town. Visitors can find out more about the story of this camp and its one-time inmates; information boards and display panels are situated around the area to explain what life in the camp was like during the 1940s.

Constructed in 1941 to provide accommodation for 4,000 prisoners of war during the Second World War, in 1949 it was converted into a training camp for the British Army, Territorial Army

and Army Cadets. During the Cold War, the Royal Observer Corps installed a nuclear monitoring post in 1960 to detect incoming atomic attack, with an underground Regional Government Headquarters built on the campsite in 1990. The Army withdrew from Cultybraggan in 2004, and the camp is now operated by Comrie Development Trust which has developed it for a variety of purposes since September 2007.

A number of the Nissen huts have been Category A and Category B listed by Historic Environment Scotland due to their national significance as of 2006. In addition to informational exhibitions detailing events at the camp during wartime (including the Cultybraggan cartoon collection – authentic pen and ink drawings created by German prisoners during the war), several of the huts have now been converted for the use of local businesses – and the process of redeveloping the camp is still ongoing. Renovation has included the supply of electricity, water, drainage and telecoms to the huts, making them suitable for a variety of commercial purposes. Renewable energy sources such as solar power and biomass heating systems are in use, a community orchard was planted in March 2010, and a variety of community allotments are also now based on the camp grounds – a pastime that has become so popular, there is now a waiting list for anyone seeking to cultivate a plot of their own. Many large-scale events also take place on the premises, including classic car rallies, and several local community groups also meet in huts on the camp grounds.

In a notable turn of events, one of the camp's former German prisoners – Heinrich Steinmeyer (1923-2013), a one-time member of the Nazi *Waffen-SS* (*Waffen Schutzstaffel*, or 'weapons protection squad') who had been incarcerated at Cultybraggan until 1948 – gifted a large sum of money to Comrie in his Last Will and Testament, which he had stated was in recognition of the compassion and humanity with which he had been

treated both during the war and as a free citizen during peacetime following his tenure as a prisoner. This bequest is now managed by a trust for the benefit of the local community.

Since the late 1960s, the town has hosted Comrie Fortnight (*www.comrie.org.uk/business-directory/95/comrie-fortnight*) – a two-week celebration between July and August consisting of many events such as a float parade, competitions and dances, with proceeds being used to support local community endeavours. The town has also become widely recognised for its torchlight flambeaux parade at Hogmanay, which includes Scottish traditional music and dancing.

Famous people born in Comrie have included Victoria Cross recipient John Manson Craig (1896-1970) who served in both World Wars, veterinary parasitologist Professor Lord Alexander Trees (1946-) and professional golfer Carly Booth (1992-), while prominent visitors to the town through the centuries have included Robert the Bruce, Mary, Queen of Scots, Rob Roy McGregor, Robert Burns, Queen Wilhemina of the Netherlands and Queen Victoria.

Braco

An ancient village which dates all the way back to antiquity, Braco is a history enthusiast's dream come true. It is particularly well-known for its proximity to the well-known Roman Fort of Ardoch (*www.undiscoveredscotland.co.uk/braco/ardochromanfort.index.html*), which was situated

just north of the existing settlement. Part of the Gask Ridge (to the north-east of Braco), it is now a scheduled monument and considered to be one of the best-preserved collection of Roman earthworks not just in Scotland, but in the entirety of the former Roman-occupied imperial territories. The fort's ditches and ramparts are still clearly visible today, and archaeologists believe that the earliest structures on the site date back to the conquest of Britain by Roman general Gnaeus Julius Agricola (40-93 AD) in the 1st century. Further fortifications were added later, and hundreds of years later a medieval chapel was built within the boundary of the fort, near what had been its centre. Prince Albert viewed the earthworks in 1842 when he visited Braco with Queen Victoria. The fort is now part of the Ardoch estate, while the Blackhill marching camp – situated to the north of the Ardoch Fort – is under the supervision of Historic Environment Scotland.

The village has become especially popular with walkers who have an interest in history, as there are many monuments and culturally significant sites based in and around Braco. These include the 18th century Ardoch Parish Church (*www.ardochparishchurch.org*) in Feddal Road, first opened for public worship in March 1781, which still has an active congregation today. Its exceptional bellcote was an 1836 addition, along with the east end chancel which was built in 1890. Nearby is the tower of Ardoch Free Church (*www.britishlistedbuildings.co.uk/200337283-free-church-tower-ardoch-ardoch*), also on Feddal Road, which was constructed in a Romanesque style in 1844 and opened in January 1845. The main building of the church was demolished after it became unsafe following a lightning strike, leaving only the tower standing. It became a Category C listed building in 1981.

Other noteworthy monuments include the Ardoch Parish War Memorial (*www.warmemorialsonline.org.uk/memorial/151728*) in Front Street, an intricate granite Celtic cross built to commemorate the lives of villagers lost during the First and Second World Wars. The village's North Park hosts another historical structure of consider-able heritage import, Ardoch Old Bridge (*www.canmore.org.uk/site/25263*), which spans the River Knaik (and is thus sometimes also known as the Knaik Bridge). The ancient, narrow pack horse bridge, which is thought to date as far back as 1430, was painstakingly restored by the Society for the Preservation of Rural Scotland in 1989. It was superseded by the village's current bridge over the Knaik, which was completed in 1862.

Braco is situated within a number of walking routes and paths winding around the Strathallan area; details are available online and from tourist information centres. Additionally, the village's picturesque Lodge Park is host to the Braco Show (*www.bracoshow.co.uk*), a well-attended outdoor agronomic event organised by the Ardoch Agricultural Society which takes place every year.

Though Braco was not formally established as a village until 1815, recently celebrating its bicentenary with a series of events in May 2015, it has nevertheless produced a number of significant public figures over the years. These have included William McGregor (1846-1911), founder of the Football League; anatomist Professor Robert Howden FRSE (1856-1940); fine artist and film-maker Ronald Forbes RSA (1947-); and videogame designer Chris Sawyer (1961-), founder of the mobile game developer 31X, who is perhaps best-known as the creator of the celebrated strategy games *Transport Tycoon* (1994) and *Rollercoaster Tycoon* (1999).

Dunblane

The centrally-located cathedral city of Dunblane, situated on the banks of the Allan Water, is a bustling community with much to see and do. Though it has become well-known in the area for its luxury hotels such as Cromlix House (*www.cromlix.com*) near Kinbuck and the Dunblane Hydro Hotel (*www.doubletreedunblane.com*) in Perth Road, the town has a great deal more to offer its visitors than opulent accommodation. It is thought that the city's name derives from 'Fort of Blane', referring to Saint Blane (?-590), a 6th century bishop who travelled to Scotland from Ireland, bringing Christian teachings to the Picts.

Topping the list of Dunblane's historical attractions is the commanding Dunblane Cathedral (*www.dunblanecathedral.org.uk*) at The Cross, which is of huge interest to architecture enthusiasts and historians alike. The town's most prominent landmark, the building is thought to have been founded on a Christian site identified with

the aforementioned Saint Blane, and it has gradually been expanded over the centuries. The lower half of its tower dates from the 11th century with its upper half added in the 15th century, while the Gothic cathedral itself was constructed around 1240, completed by Bishop Clement (?-1258). The entire building was comprehensively restored by Victorian architect Rowand Anderson FRSE, RSA (1834-1921) between 1889 and 1893.

Home to a large congregation comprising around a thousand members, the cathedral organises a number of community services and events – including several worship services at various times throughout the week. It has a long musical tradition, including a choir and handbell ringers, and is especially renowned for its cathedral organ which was built by Netherlands-based Flentrop of Zaandam in 1990. A number of musical concerts are staged at the cathedral throughout the year; check their website for details of their schedule. While Dunblane Cathedral is part of the Church of Scotland, Historic Environment Scotland is custodian of the building. Entrance is free of charge to members of the public. Please note, however, that as the cathedral is a working place of worship, there are occasions – such as weddings, christenings and funerals – where access will temporarily be unavailable.

Located nearby, also at The Cross, is Dunblane Museum (*www.dunblanemuseum.org.uk*), which was established in 1943. It relates the history of Dunblane over the centuries, including the fascinating story of the construction of the cathedral. There is a wealth of history on display, with

star exhibits including a four thousand-year old necklace that was excavated near the city, an immense collection of around 6,000 communion tokens (the oldest dating back to 1648), and a social history exhibition detailing items of significance to Dunblane from centuries ago right up to the recent past. The building in which the museum is situated provides a fascinating insight into Dunblane's past in its own right; dating back to 1624, it was once the residence of the Dean of Dunblane Cathedral (later a butcher's store and then a science laboratory) before being converted into its current form in 1943. The museum building is now owned by the Society of Friends of Dunblane Cathedral, while the museum itself is operated by a Board of Trustees and a dedicated team of volunteers.

Also well worth visiting in The Cross is the Leighton Library (*www.leightonlibrary.org.uk*), the oldest purpose-built library in Scotland. The library was founded from the bequest of Bishop Robert Leighton (1611-84), who bequeathed his

collection of books and savings with the plan of constructing a building to house them in Dunblane, so that they could be consulted by members of the city's clergy. In addition to being appointed Bishop of Dunblane by King Charles II (1630-85), Leighton was also Principal of the University of Edinburgh. From Leighton's initial gift of 1,400 books, the collection has increased over the centuries to comprise around 4,500 volumes printed in an estimated 89 different languages. These include a first edition of Sir Walter Scott's influential narrative poem *The Lady of the Lake* (1810), a book of poetry by historian George Buchanan (1506-82) and a prayer book belonging to Lady Jane Grey (1537-54), amongst innumerable other works of interest. The building is open on particular dates and times between May and September, so sightseers and book lovers may want to check opening times ahead of their visit in order to avoid disappointment.

Visitors to Dunblane are sure to enjoy the quirky historical sight of Queen Victoria's Horse-shoe (*www.dunblane.info/community-2/item-/148-queen-victorias-horseshoe*) – an eccentric piece of the preserved past at the corner of Bridgend and Stirling Road, where a horseshoe thrown from one of Queen Victoria's royal horses – when her carriage passed through the city in 1842 – was attached to the wall for posterity after local blacksmith Mr McKenzie reshod the horse in question. A commemorative plaque marks the spot. According to local legend, anyone who rubs the horseshoe will be blessed with good luck.

Along with its eclectic shopping centre, full of colourful independent stores, Dunblane is well-regarded for its range of walks – foremost among them being the famed Dunblane Heritage Walk (*www.dunblane.info/public-services/library/1448-walks-dunblane*), which invites visitors to view thousands of years of history with an amble through this picturesque city. There are no less than 35 separate locations on the walk, so be sure to pick up a copy of the information leaflet which accompanies it, produced by the Dunblane Local History Society (*www.dunblane.info/item/361-dunblane-local-history-society*). Other popular walking destinations around the town include nearby Holme Hill, which is believed to be the one-time site of the monastery founded by Saint Blane in the 7th century; the Faery Footbridge over the Allan Water, built in 1911; and the city's war memorial, the Dunblane and Lecropt Cenotaph at the Haugh, designed by architect James Miller FRSE, RSA (1860-1947). Unveiled in October 1921 and rededicated in 1948, the monument commemorates lives lost in the defence of the country during wartime. There are a great many fascinating locations to visit around the city, several of them reflecting its long connection with religious history.

For younger visitors, there is the well-maintained children's play area at Laigh Hills Park (*www.dunblane.info/dcc/item/145-laigh-hills*), a well-used ground which features football pitches, swings and a skate park, the latter being constructed thanks to a community fundraising initiative. Laigh Hills Park is also the perfect place for nature admirers, with many walks around an area filled with interesting varieties of flora and fauna. The Dunblane Centre (*www.dunblanecentre.co.uk*) in Stirling Road is the city's fitness and leisure centre, offering activities to suit every age from pre-schoolers through to adults. Alongside physical training such as martial arts, athletics and pilates, there are also many other activities such as ballet, aerial skills, meditation and music instruction. Ad-

ditionally, there are numerous events taking place at the centre through the year, as well as drama classes, a community choir and an outdoor community space. Have a look at their website for information about their full range of pursuits. Based in Perth Road is the Dunblane New Golf Club (*www.dngc.co.uk*), founded in 1922 and formally opened in June 1924 as a successor to the city's original Golf Club (a 9-hole course which had been based at what is now the Laigh Hills Park). The Club has gone from strength to strength since then, and in addition to their well-regarded 18-hole parkland course – which was designed by James Braid and Major Cecil Hutchison – the club also has excellent hospitality facilities and conferencing services. Visitors should check the website ahead of time for details of green fees and other information.

Dunblane also contains a true historical curiosity in the form of a wartime replica of the German Atlantic Wall (*www.atlanticwalls.uk*) near Sheriffmuir Road, constructed to train Allied

soldiers in assaulting heavily-fortified emplacements during the Second World War. The original Atlantic Wall had been a plan by Nazi Germany, implemented by the German engineering body *Organisation Todt*, to buttress coastal defences from Norway to Spain with a solid concrete wall that was expected to deter the Allies from mounting an invasion. The Atlantic Wall was constructed between 1942 and 1944, and Allied intelligence eventually ascertained the composition, structure and dimensions of the wall which enabled them to replicate 'mock-ups' for drilling troops prior to the 1944 D-Day invasion as well as testing its resistance to attack. The replica at the Sheriffmuir Hills location gives some indication of the sheer scale of the original wall; a fascinating yet chilling remnant from Europe's darkest hour. The Atlantic Wall replica near Dunblane is the only one of its kind thought to survive in Scotland, though three others can be found in England (in Surrey, Suffolk and Essex) as well as one in Wales (in Pembrokeshire).

Another intriguing enigma at the heart of Dunblane is Scotland's Secret Chapel (*www.old-churcheshouse.com/chapel*), located near the Old Churches House Hotel in Cathedral Square. The site of the current hotel, which was once an ecumenical conference centre, was being renovated in 1960 when a previously-unknown chapel was uncovered during building work. It is thought that the room was once a 13th century place of Christian worship, and has been meticulously restored by experts to preserve it for future generations. With

its stone walls and rounded ceiling, the chapel provides a captivating glimpse into a bygone time and remains a tranquil place of peace for any visitor seeking to get away from the hustle and bustle of everyday life. Admission to the chapel is free.

During your stay in Dunblane, don't forget to visit the gold Royal Mail pillar box in the town's High Street. It was painted in its current distinctive hue in 2012 to celebrate the achievement of sporting hero Sir Andy Murray OBE (1987-), two-time Wimbledon champion, winning the Tennis Gold Medal at the London Olympics that year. Though born in Glasgow – as was his brother, Grand Slam-winning doubles player Jamie Murray OBE (1986-) – Sir Andy grew up in Dunblane and became a well-known figure in the city. In addition to winning the ATP World Tour Finals and the Davis Cup, he was to earn Olympic Gold for a second time in 2016, and many exhibits from his hugely successful tennis career are now on display in Dunblane Museum.

While Sir Andy may arguably be Dunblane's most famous son these days, the city has produced many other well-known figures over the years. These have included legal expert Patrick James Stirling FRSE (1809-91); architect James Gillespie Graham (1776-1855); Victoria Cross winner Major James Palmer Huffam (1897-1968), who served in both World Wars; and music legend Dougie MacLean OBE (1954-).

Bridge of Allan

Situated close to Stirling, the scenic town of Bridge of Allan boasts many independent shops and businesses which are always popular with tourists. The settlement dates back as far as the Iron Age, though the clachans (or hamlets) which formed the basis of the town we recognise today were formally recognised collectively as a village by a Royal Charter dating back to 1146. Bridge of Allan stretches from the University of Stirling campus to the Allan Water towards Logie; a stone bridge over the River Allan was constructed in 1520, with mining operations for precious metals taking place in the area from the 16th century. The Jacobites occupied the town in 1745 and took possession of its bridge, charging crossing fees. One of the toll posts that they set up can still be seen today.

Bridge of Allan was developed as a spa town in the 19th century when the Laird of Westerton, Major John Alexander Henderson (1806-58), designed ambitious plans in 1850 to modernise the existing village (which at the time largely consisted of traditional thatched cottages) and develop it into an attractive contemporary town which would attract visitors during the boom in hydropathic

excursions at the time. Henderson is now essentially considered the creator of modern Bridge of Allan, and the main street which runs through the town has been named in his honour. It was Henderson who made plans for the town's Fountain of Ninevah (*www.holeousia.com/time-passes-listen/bridge-of-allan/the-fountain-of-ninevah/*) to be constructed on Fountain Road in 1853. Its heron statue, which perches high upon its apex, was added in 1895. While the fountain is no longer in full working order, it has been scrupulously repainted in recent years and remains one of the town's most famous sights.

Henderson envisaged a thoroughly modern town with wide, commodious streets and a pleasure ground to be established in nearby woodland. The town became an independent burgh in 1870, and retains many of the Victorian villas and grand public buildings from this golden age. Visitors today can still visit prominent landmarks from the town's earlier days, including the Paterson Memorial Clock (*www.memorialdrinkingfountains.word-press.com/2017/08/20/paterson-memorial-clock/*), a 12-foot high public clock and drinking fountain in the centre of the town's Henderson Street which

was built in 1898 in memory of eminent local figure Dr Alexander Paterson (1822-98), the burgh's long-serving Medical Officer of Health and Justice of the Peace who was also a keen horticulturalist and highly experienced antiquary. Constructed from a design by the pioneering sculptor Alexander 'Greek' Thomson (1817-75), it is of national significance and was extensively restored in 2009.

Another admired venue for visitors is the beautiful Pullar Memorial Park, a peaceful area of parkland on Henderson Street which was founded in 1923 by philanthropic industrialist Edmund Pullar (1848-1926) as a location for the town's War Memorial (*www.warmemorialsonline.org.uk/memorial/116935*). Edmund Pullar was the brother of geographer and businessman Laurence Pullar FRSE (1837-1926), and son of John Pullar (1803-78), the eminent founder of J&J Pullar Ltd. – better-known as simply Pullars of Perth, dry cleaners and dyeworks.

Famous people to be born in Bridge of Allan include steamship captain and Hawaii politician Captain James A. King (1832-99); Victoria Cross recipient Lt. Colonel William Eagleson Gordon CBE (1866-1941); and TV personality Judy Murray OBE (1959-), tennis coach and mother of Jamie and Sir Andy Murray. Novelist Robert Louis Stevenson was a regular visitor to Bridge of Allan throughout his early life during the 19th century.

The town is home to the popular Bridge of Allan Golf Club (*www.bofagc.com*) on Pendreich Road, with its attractive 9-hole course which dates back to 1895 and the design of Old Tom Morris. The course boasts stunning views of the surrounding Stirlingshire countryside and Stirling Castle, with plenty of challenging play. Online booking is available for visitors, so checking the website for current green fees and other information is recommended. Visitors can also check in at the Allan Centre Sports Hall (*www.stirling.gov.uk/community-leisure/book-a-centre-or-hall/allan-centre/*), the town's well-used leisure facility on Fountain Road which houses a games hall, lounge and PE room, and is regularly used for indoors sports, community activities, public meetings and training events.

Bridge of Allan's annual Highland Games (*www.bofagames.com*) take place at Strathallan Games Park every August, and were originally initiated by Major Henderson in 1862. Sporting events include wrestling, athletics, cycling and heavyweight eventing, while the Games have also become well-known for their highland dancing and pipe bands. The event is a hugely popular local attraction, and a number of prizes and trophies are awarded to winning participants every year.

One especially well-liked destination in town is the Allanwater Brewhouse (*www.allanwater-brewhouse.co.uk*) on Queens Lane, which offers tasting sessions and information about the brewing process in a welcoming and comfortable environment. Established in 1996 by Douglas Ross, the brewery has proven to be enduringly successful with a huge variety of brews on sale ranging from the traditional to the experimental. Some of their more remarkable flavours include marmalade, lavender, rhubarb and ginger, Earl Grey tea, beetroot and black pepper, and even Christmas pudding! Tours of the brewery can be booked, with a variety of trips on offer. The bar is especially

popular with visitors, with a great opportunity to socialise as well as sampling the products on offer. Many events take place at the Brewhouse, including quiz nights and beer festivals, though it has become particularly well-known for its music nights where a fantastic range of live music artists play on the premises.

A surprising but little-known fact is that The Beatles once performed at Bridge of Allan (*www.beatlesbible.com/1963/01/05/live-museum-hall-bridge-of-allan-scotland*); the Fab Four played on stage at Henderson Street's Museum Hall in January 1963, the penultimate venue of their tour of Scotland. Bridge of Allan Museum Hall was built in 1887, initially as the Macfarlane Museum and Art Gallery, but closed down in 1978 along with its public auditorium. It has since been converted into private residential apartments, though the grand exterior of the building (which overlooks Pullar Memorial Park) can still be seen to this day.

Private day tours around the town's historical landmarks can be arranged from Outlandish Journeys (*www.outlandishjourneys.com*), guided by a knowledgeable professional historian and genealogist, providing an experience which will cover a comprehensive range of facts about the local area and beyond. For those seeking to go exploring the area on their own, Strathallan Community Rail Partnership (*www.strathallancrp.org.uk*) has produced a number of informational leaflets outlining walking routes with Bridge of Allan as their nucleus, featuring nearby destinations such as Dunblane, Dumyat and Carse of Lecropt. Many other rambling routes are available.

Walkers will also find much to enjoy on the University of Stirling campus (*www.stir.ac.uk*), regularly considered to be among the most scenic in all of Europe, where people are free to can take in the sights of beautiful Airthrey Loch – the focal point of the university grounds. A wander around the extensive Airthrey Estate, within which the campus is based, is highly recommended, and the grounds contain a significant variety of flora and fauna. Founded in 1967, Stirling University has

become particularly well-known for its sporting facilities, which include the National Swimming Academy, the Gannochy National Tennis Centre, the 9-hole Airthrey Golf Course, playing fields, and many sporting facilities including a fitness centre, racquet sport courts, and many other services. A major interdisciplinary university, a number of specialist research centres are based on the campus. Additionally, Stirling University's Pathfoot Building was used as the filming location of the fictional 'Inverness College' in *Outlander*'s season 2, while the iconic glass walkway between the Cottrell Building and the Atrium was employed as a location in season 4 – where it performed the unusual function of doubling for a concourse at Boston Logan International Airport in Massachusetts!

Stirling University campus is also the location of the Macrobert Arts Centre (*www.macrobertartscentre.org*), which houses a variety of live performance spaces and cinema screens. Originally the concept of the university's founding

Principal, chemist Professor Tom Cottrell FRSE (1923-73), who was a passionate supporter of culture and the arts, the centre opened in 1971 and has been extensively renovated and upgraded in recent years. It is now well-known throughout the area for its diverse programme of events, which include dance, stand-up comedy, exhibitions, music, live theatre and opera. Check ahead to consult their schedule and see what's taking place, as there is never a shortage of experiences at the Macrobert.

Just a short drive away from Bridge of Allan is the city of Stirling, meaning that the Heart 200 circuit is complete. However, the road trip is really just the beginning of your travels through Central Scotland, for there are so many towns and villages that are just off the main route which are equally worthy of your time and attention. This book gives just the merest taste of the history and culture of this amazing region, and visitors are invited to 'jump on' at any point of the map, pick out a series of mini-trips – or even travel the whole route in reverse order! The guide is just the beginning of your adventures on the most exciting road trip that Scotland has to offer.

Photo Credits

The illustrations in this book are sourced from the personal photographic collection of the authors, with the exception of the following images which are detailed below:

Page 2: Stirling Castle on Castle Hill. Photo by DerWeg at Pixabay. Public domain image.

Page 2: Stirling Castle Portcullis. Photo by Walkerssk at Pixabay. Public domain image.

Page 3: Stirling Castle Interior Grounds. Photo by Almu at Pixabay. Public domain image.

Page 4: The King's Knot. Photo by Walkerssk at Pixabay. Public domain image.

Page 4: The National Wallace Monument on Abbey Craig. Photo by Sophia Hilmar at Pixabay. Public domain image.

Page 5: Detail of the National Wallace Monument. Photo by Greg Montani at Pixabay. Public domain image.

Page 5: Exterior of the Stirling Smith Art Gallery and Museum. Image Copyright © The Stirling Smith Art Gallery and Museum, all rights reserved, and reproduced by kind permission of the copyright holder.

Page 6: The World's Oldest Football display at the Stirling Smith Art Gallery and Museum. Image Copyright © The Stirling Smith Art Gallery and Museum, all rights reserved, and reproduced by kind permission of the copyright holder.

Page 7: Stirling Old Bridge. Photo by Sophia Hilmar at Pixabay. Public domain image.

Page 8: King Robert the Bruce Statue. Photo by Sophia Hilmar at Pixabay. Public domain image.

Page 10: Detail of Statue of John Cowane at Cowane's Hospital, Stirling. Image Copyright © Dr Murray Cook, all rights reserved, and reproduced by kind permission of the copyright holder.

Page 11: Interior of the Church of the Holy Rude, Stirling. Photo by anciaes at Pixabay. Public domain image.

Page 11: Panorama of the Valley Cemetery, Stirling. Photo by Kamyq at Pixabay. Public domain image.

Page 17: The Beheading Stone at Mote Hill, Stirling. Image Copyright © Dr Murray Cook, all rights reserved, and reproduced by kind permission of the copyright holder.

Page 20: Big Cats at Blair Drummond Safari Park. Image Copyright © Blair Drummond Safari Park, all rights reserved, and reproduced by kind permission of the copyright holder.

Page 20: Giraffes at Blair Drummond Safari Park. Image Copyright © Blair Drummond Safari Park, all rights reserved, and reproduced by kind permission of the copyright holder.

Page 21: Duncarron Medieval Village. Image Copyright © Duncarron Medieval Village and the Clanranald Trust for Scotland, all rights reserved, and reproduced by kind permission of the copyright holder.

About the Authors

DR THOMAS CHRISTIE has many years of experience as a literary and publishing professional, working in collaboration with several companies including Cambridge Scholars Publishing, Crescent Moon Publishing, Robert Greene Publishing and Applause Books. A passionate advocate of the written word and literary arts, over the years he has worked to develop original writing for respected organisations such as the Stirling Smith Art Gallery and Museum and a leading independent higher education research unit based at the University of Stirling. Additionally, he is regularly involved in public speaking events and has delivered guest lectures and presentations about his work at many locations around the United Kingdom. He is co-director of Extremis Publishing.

Tom was elected a Fellow of the Royal Society of Arts in 2018, and is a member of the Royal Society of Literature, the Society of Authors, the Federation of Writers Scotland and the Authors' Licensing and Collecting Society. He holds a first-class Honours degree in English Literature and a Master's degree in Humanities with British Cinema History from the Open University in Milton Keynes, and a Doctorate in Scottish Literature awarded by the University of Stirling.

He is the author of a number of books on the subject of modern film which include *Liv Tyler: Star in Ascendance* (2007), *The Cinema of Richard Linklater* (2008), *John Hughes and Eighties Cinema: Teenage Hopes and American Dreams* (2009), *Ferris Bueller's Day Off: Pocket Movie Guide* (2010), *The Christmas Movie Book* (2011), *The James Bond Movies of the 1980s* (2013), *Mel Brooks: Genius and Loving It!: Freedom and Liberation in the Cinema of Mel Brooks* (2015), *A Righteously Awesome Eighties Christmas: Festive Cinema of the 1980s* (2016), *John Hughes FAQ* (2019) and *The Golden Age of Christmas Movies: Festive Cinema of the 1940s and 50s* (2019).

His other works include *Notional Identities: Ideology, Genre and National Identity in Popular Scottish Fiction Since the Seventies* (2013), *The Spectrum of Adventure: A Brief History of Interactive Fiction on the Sinclair ZX Spectrum* (2016), and *Contested Mindscapes: Exploring Approaches to Dementia in Modern Popular Culture* (2018). He has also written a crowdfunded murder-mystery novel, *The Shadow in the Gallery* (2013), which is set during the nineteenth century in Stirling's historic Smith Art Gallery and Museum.

For more details about Tom and his work, please visit his website at: **www.tomchristiebooks.co.uk**

JULIE CHRISTIE has been working in different roles within business and the third sector for more than three decades. Over the years she has worked with a number of charitable organisations such as the Princess Royal Trust for Carers, the Aberlour Childcare Trust, the Alzheimer's Society, the Royal Voluntary Service and Town Break Dementia Care. She was also an associate with the University of Stirling, where she was involved in the development of Dementia Friendly Communities. Julie is currently the Communities and Fund-raising Manager for Start Up Stirling, the city's food bank.

She brings considerable experience from the commercial retail industry, having held posts with national organisations including AstraZeneca, the NHS, Marks and Spencer, Goldsmiths, Thorntons and Laura Ashley. She holds a Bachelor of Nursing degree from the University of Glasgow and a Bachelor of Science degree with first-class Honours in Sociology and Social Policy from the Open University, which she loved doing as it concentrated on the things that fascinated her about people and culture as well as exploring how we can both see the same thing and yet hold an entirely different point of view.

Her hardest job was dealing with fraught brides when she worked in the wedding trade, where she had to develop her tea-making skills as well as occasionally mopping up tears! The most rewarding job of all – and also the worst-paid – was looking after her late Mum, who had to live with many chronic illnesses.

Julie had never tried being self-employed, so – given her passion for lifelong learning and literacy – the next logical step was to co-found a publishing business, Extremis Publishing Ltd., with her brother Tom. By roping him in to her grand plan, they were able to bring different life skills to the mix. The company specialises in arts, media and culture non-fiction, and their mission is to provide an eclectic range of interesting books, continuing in the long heritage of publishing in the city of Stirling. She is convinced that real life is always more interesting than fiction. *The Heart 200 Book* is her first published work.

Her view on life is that you should never be afraid to try new things, everyone should have a fair chance, that living life is way more interesting than doing the dusting, and that she has never found a box of chocolates that she hasn't liked yet!

Digging into Stirling's Past
Uncovering the Secrets of Scotland's Smallest City

By Murray Cook

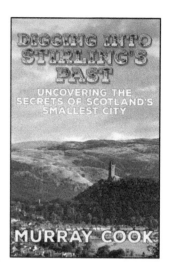

Stirling is Scotland's smallest city and one of its newest. But, strangely, it's also the ancient capital and one of the most important locations in all of Scottish history. If you wanted to invade or to resist invasion, you did it at Stirling. It has witnessed Celts, Romans, Britons, Picts, Scots, Angles, Vikings, Edward I, William Wallace, Robert the Bruce, Edward II, Oliver Cromwell, Bonnie Prince Charlie, the Duke of Cumberland, and even played a decisive role in D-Day.

This huge history has left its mark all over this tiny place. Stirling is Scotland's best preserved medieval city, boasting one of Europe's finest Renaissance palaces, the world's oldest football, Mary Queen of Scots' coronation, James III's grave and murder scene, the site of a successful 16th century assassination of Scotland's head of state, Scotland's first powered and unpowered flights, Scotland's biggest royal rubbish dump, one of

Scotland's earliest churches, Scotland's two most important battles, vitrified forts, Scotland's oldest and best preserved Royal Park, connections to King Arthur and the Vikings, Britain's last beheading, Scotland's largest pyramid – and its oldest resident is 4000 years old!

This book tells Stirling's story through its secret nooks and crannies; the spots the tourists overlook and those that the locals have forgotten or never visited. Join Stirling's Burgh Archaeologist, Dr Murray Cook, as he takes you on a tour of a fascinating city's history which is full of heroes and battles, grave robbing, witch trials, bloody beheadings, violent sieges, Jacobite plots, assassins, villains, plagues, Kings and Queens... and much, much more besides.

The Grocer's Boy
A Slice of His Life in 1950s Scotland

By Robert Murray

The 1950s in Carnoustie: a beautiful seaside town on the Tayside coast, and a place which was to see rapid social and technological advancement during one of the fastest-moving periods of cultural change in recent British history.

In *The Grocer's Boy*, Robert Murray relates his account of an eventful childhood in post-War Scotland, drawing on fond memories of his loving family, his droll and often mischievous group of friends, and the many inspirational people who influenced him and helped to shape his early life.

Join Robert on his adventures in retail as he advances from his humble beginnings as a delivery boy for the famous William Low grocery firm, all the way to becoming the youngest manager in the company's history at just nineteen years of age. Read tales of his hectic, hard-working time as an apprentice grocer – sometimes humorous, occasionally nerve-wracking, but never less than entertaining.

From Robert's early romances and passion for stage performance to his long-running battle of wits with his temperamental delivery bike, *The Grocer's Boy* is a story of charm and nostalgia; the celebration of a happy youth in a distinctive bygone age.

For details of new and forthcoming books from Extremis Publishing, including our podcasts, please visit our official website at:

www.extremispublishing.com

or follow us on social media at:

www.facebook.com/extremispublishing

www.linkedin.com/company/extremis-publishing-ltd-/

Lightning Source UK Ltd.
Milton Keynes UK
UKHW050202260920
370527UK00003B/22

9 781999 696214